Evaluating Acquisitions and Collection Management

Forthcoming Topics in *The Acquisitions Librarian* series:

• Acquisitions and Resource Sharing, Number 7
• Gifts and Exchanges, Number 8
• Serials Acquisitions, Number 9
• Acquisitions and Collection Development Policies, Number 10
• The Collections Manager, and Training of Acquisitions Librarians, Number 11
• Acquisitions of Popular Culture Materials, Number 12

Note: The order of the series is subject to change

Evaluating Acquisitions and Collection Management

Edited by
Pamela S. Cenzer
Cynthia I. Gozzi

The Haworth Press
New York • London • Sydney

Evaluating Acquisitions and Collection Management has also been published as *The Acquisitions Librarian,* Number 6 1991 (Volume 3).

The Haworth Press, Inc., 10 Alice Street, Binghamton, NY 13904-1580
EUROSPAN/Haworth, 3 Henrietta Street, London WC2E 8LU England
ASTAM/Haworth, 162-168 Parramatta Road, Stanmore (Sydney), N. S. W. 2048 Australia

Library of Congress Cataloging-in-Publication Data

Evaluating acquisitions and collection management / edited by Pamela S. Cenzer, Cynthia I. Gozzi.
    p. cm.
    "Has also been published as The Acquisitions librarian, number 6, 1991" — T.p. verso.
    ISBN 1-56024-160-8 (acid-free paper)
    1. Collection development (Libraries) — Evaluation. 2. Acquisitions (Libraries) — Evaluation. I. Cenzer, Pamela S. II. Gozzi, Cynthia I.
Z687.E9 1991
025.2'1 — dc20

                                                  91-15299
                                                    CIP

Evaluating Acquisitions and Collection Management

CONTENTS

EVALUATING SPECIFIC ACQUISITIONS PROCESSES

ABOUT THE EDITORS

Pamela Cenzer, MLS, is currently Selector for the Physical Sciences at Marston Science Library, University of Florida at Gainesville. She has fifteen years of research library experience, ten of which have been in acquisitions or collection development. Ms. Cenzer belongs to the American Library Association, ACLIS, and ACRL.

Cynthia Gozzi, MA, MLS, is Associate Director of Technical Services/Libraries & Information Resources at Stanford University in California. A native of Australia, Ms. Gozzi came to Stanford in 1981. Previously she held positions at the State University of New York and Syracuse University. She has published a range of articles and is a popular speaker on topics ranging from local systems, designs, and costs to the future of technical services. She is an active member of the American Library Association, the Research Libraries Group, and the Coalition for Networked Information.

Introduction

Pamela S. Cenzer
Cynthia I. Gozzi

Among the characteristics of good management are evidence of planning and ongoing evaluation of programs. Among the characteristics of a good plan, one usually finds an evaluative phase. No project, no matter how ingenious or innovative, will be granted support by a funding agency without a solid evaluation plan. Why is evaluation so strongly recommended and held in such high regard? Partially it is regarded as an insurance policy for the wise use of resources and as a mechanism for insuring that either wise decisions have been made or that, if they prove to be unwise, adjustments are identified and implemented. In the worst of cases, I suspect, evaluation is engaged in as part of some "neat and tidy syndrome."

In mathematics, evaluation means to express in numerical terms. Numbers offer convenient, concise and commonly agreed upon measures of relative value. However, few library management issues can be adequately described by a spreadsheet. Authors of papers in this volume describe a variety of evaluation activities that cover both qualitative and quantitative approaches.

Research libraries exist in dynamic environments. Virtually none of the functions performed in libraries can be considered in a meaningful way if the institutional context is ignored. The first section of this issue contains articles that explore current trends and the impact on collection development and acquisitions. Collections are the lasting result of acquisitions and collection development activity. As such, the evaluation of collections can reveal patterns of program support that can be compared between peer institutions. Treadwell and Spornick document a successful strategy for using evaluation to win more resources.

Acquisitions processes may appear uncomplicated to the uniniti-

1

ated. Authors belie this impression as they discuss the balancing act of acquisitions in the collection development process as well as the increasing emphasis on services to library users. This quality of acquisitions work is essential but nearly impossible to measure. This service component is addressed by Sugnet and Bosch, Fleishauer and McSweeney, and Chamberlain. Alsbury considers the services of an acquisitions department to be similar to vendor-supplied services, a model that illustrates the need to consider organizational context. In an insightful case study approach, Palm and Reich describe the process of assigning relative value to acquisitions activities at Stanford University following a natural and budgetary disaster.

Performance appraisal is considered by both Edwards and Angiletta. Individuals contribute in unique ways to the evolving organization. Angiletta comments on the organizational realities surrounding the evaluation process of collection developers.

Finally, two authors describe parts of the process of acquiring materials and methods for improving procedures. Clark writes about the initial stages of bibliographic verification while Ogburn and Rice conclude with fund accounting. Both articles acknowledge the need for ongoing revision and evaluation of procedures.

This collection of papers, while loosely linked to an evaluative theme, is not meant to provide an exhaustive coverage of the topic. The editors set out to be "neat and tidy" and had expected that we would receive articles on use studies, organizational studies, evaluative methodologies, and evaluative criteria. Instead, individual authors combined the terms collection development/acquisitions and evaluation and produced less predictable results. We were intrigued by the range of interests and experiences expressed in the articles.

We wish to acknowledge with immense gratitude the production assistance given us by Angela Jarchow and Lisa Carlson of the Stanford University Libraries.

THE CONTEXT

Complement or Contradiction:
The Role of Acquisitions
in the Access versus Ownership
Dynamic

Greg Anderson

SUMMARY. There are many issues affecting academic libraries which question our fundamental role and function within the scholarly community. This article examines the issues related to the strategic visions of access or ownership which confront each library and offers a proposal to begin exploration of opportunities.

INTRODUCTION

Myriad factors bring the issue of access vs. ownership into the academic library: an invigorated service commitment to our scholarly communities; a continuum of investigating and understanding the economics of scholarship in the 90's; strategic planning—"that

Greg Anderson is Associate Director for Systems and Planning, MIT Libraries, 14S-216, Cambridge, MA 02139.

3

vision thing" — for academic librarianship; and, weaving the warp and woof of information technologies into the fabric of our professional lives. Discussions of these factors have centered primarily upon the public service and collections functions. These same factors, however, bring considerable focus upon the role of acquisitions in our organizations. This discussion will define and frame some of the issues, questions, challenges, opportunities, and new directions for acquisitions.

DEFINITIONS: ACCESS AND OWNERSHIP

Access versus ownership trips glibly from many tongues these days, and the phrase is often received with perspicacious head nodding. We each construct private definitions of issues such as this; for example, do we share a consensus definition of "information technologies" or "scholarly communications?" This discussion will treat access as those activities in which we engage to connect our clients with knowledge, and ownership will be held as the physical possession of the various media containing knowledge. Access and ownership intersect at the point of knowledge identification and service; they differ in that access implies facilitation between the client and knowledge regardless of physical location or ownership. This gateway approach to transferring information does not mean that the library is a catalyst because the knowledge transaction is affected by the library, and the library's approach to this service alters it in a fundamental way. Ownership connotes an organized, cohesively constructed archive of knowledge artifacts — access to and use of this knowledge are physically connected.

Access implies a distributed, de-centralized approach to knowledge identification and procurement; ownership implies a central collection and organization of knowledge. In a broader context, one could consider whether the library and its collections remain the center of the university or if the library and its access to knowledge are another "node" in the campus information environment. In both environments there remains a distinction between access to and delivery of information.

Why this issue now? The concept of the library as an archive of knowledge is under scrutiny for a variety of reasons: technology, especially the evolving network structures and opportunities in higher education; duplicative collections, their maintenance and costs; economics (can we and our administrations afford multiple comprehensive collections?); and, the information glut, especially in non-traditional or electronic media. In the Knowledge Executive, Harlan Cleveland offers some valuable characteristics of information which are challenging and shaping the way libraries work:

1. Information is expandable
2. Information is compressible
3. Information is substitutable
4. Information is transportable
5. Information is diffusive
6. Information is shareable

> The information resource, in short, is different in kind from other resources. And that's important because information has become our key resource.[1]

What does this have to do with acquisitions? Everything. The skills, traditions, and values of acquisitions departments poise them uniquely to be major players in the emerging interplay of access and ownership.

FUNCTION VERSUS ORGANIZATIONS

Assuming this major role requires some initial introspection; what are the programs and activities which acquisitions supports within the library, the academic institution, and within higher education and the social evolution fabric of the country? While this may sound too abstract and heady, the realization of the acquisitions function as a fundamental contribution to research, public service, accreditation, teaching and curriculum, and the social, cultural sustenance which characterizes the journey of life-long learning helps broaden the perspective beyond the organizational box traditionally residing in technical services.

If we agree to look at acquisitions this way, we can then approach other, similar activities which normally reside elsewhere in the library. For libraries which embrace an access orientation, the distinction between acquisition of materials and information brokering begins to fade. The acquisitions department is skilled at vendor relations and negotiations. Does the knowledge medium require a different organizational structure? Are we following procedural complexity (which acquisitions handles superbly) with organizational complexity?

SERVICE VERSUS TRADITION

Acquisitions departments normally handle procurement of print media, microforms, and now, some electronic media such as CD-ROM. The complexity of such a task has been validated:

> At the University of North Carolina, for example, a CPA management consultant from the University's Systems and Procedures Department conducted a three-person, month-long study of the Acquisitions Department. He concluded that it was easily the most complex procurement operation he had ever examined. Even more gratifying was his conclusion that the department's procedural complexity was fully justified by the demands of acquiring library materials from an international market in a research library environment.[2]

In both ownership and access libraries the question must be raised: Why not exploit that talent to deal with this procedural and multi-layered complexity more broadly? The skills of acquisitions staff to work effectively with vendors and the community outside the libraries are valuable commodities. Why not have acquisitions negotiate on-line subscriptions to commercial databases? Document delivery services? Regardless of format, the function is to serve knowledge to our clients, a function which is well established procedurally within acquisitions. Organizationally the library then accomplishes coordination and streamlining while recognizing and utilizing the procedural skills necessary for success.

The access/ownership dynamic encourages us to look at ourselves more creatively: we focus on function rather than organization, on content rather than medium, and on services rather than tradition.

THE LIBRARY VERSUS ITS INSTITUTION

Most academic libraries fulfill a central mission on the campus: acquiring, organizing, servicing, and preserving knowledge for the use of the community. Based upon the culture of the institution those collections may be comprehensive or tightly focused for the points of excellence that school supports. Maintaining an ownership model represents a status quo stance for the library—if it ain't broke, don't fix it. As institutions look toward relatively flat growth, opportunities for indirect cost recovery, moderate tuition growth, inflation rates for materials, the burden on the institution's operating budget, personnel costs, and program scrutiny, the ownership model becomes highly visible and questionable. Ownership oriented libraries, however, can point to cohesive services, including access to and delivery of knowledge; they can also trot out quantitative statistics which institution administrators can understand and value as comparative measures with peer institutions.

The ownership model does not preclude new directions for acquisitions; organizational streamlining and utilization of acquisitions expertise are valid areas of development in both the access and ownership environments.

Access oriented libraries confront a different set of problems and opportunities. The problems are largely tradition- and values-based; how does an archiving library re-create itself with an access oriented model? Very carefully. Mary Ann Griffin states that: "Values provide guidelines to interpret the significance to an individual of certain happenings."[3] The goals of an organization should be reflective of its values. If an organization decides to pursue an access orientation, it must carefully assess its current goals and values and promote and inculcate the new access values which it wishes to embrace. Without this thoughtfully crafted foundation a new access orientation will fail, because the organization has not internalized and validated access as a goal. Other problems for access libraries include a high degree of dependence on cooperative programs such as ILL, persuading the institution administration that quantitative statistics are not critical to library rankings, and, conversely, demonstrating to the institution that access promotes the qualitative servicing of knowledge and that programs are in fact more successful. To continue support for the institution's programs and curriculum, how do the Library and the acquisitions department determine the critical mass of materials to support the institution's mission? This issue is especially critical for accreditation procedures and, of course, for the local collection demands for faculty. How much duplication of materials across libraries is tolerable from the institution's viewpoint; from the Library's; from publishers'? What are the possible influences on intellectual property rights if the volume of publications falls because of reduced buying by the access libraries?

Finally, the library will need to anticipate and address frustrations of clients who have access to knowledge — they know it exists because of the library services, but they may not be able to get their hands on the knowledge in a timely manner. The integration of access and delivery is a major shared concern for libraries.

The opportunities presented in an access orientation include becoming an information technology leader on campus, focusing more resources on the individual knowledge requirements of clients, participating in the issues made visible by the national and international networks, and providing direct connections between costs and services. With proper monitoring and measuring tools, we may be able to assess the qualitative success of our programs.

Acquisitions will be faced with an entirely new set of demands in this environment, although the characteristics of complexity and interactions beyond the libraries will continue and increase. Staff will be faced with a severe learning curve; understanding the implications and structures of networked information sources is a challenge. Forging strong cooperative agreements with other institutions will be critical, and this will herald a move from the relative isolation of acquisitions departments as "front-ends" in the knowledge gathering process to a continuous, integrated involvement at multiple points. Learning the nuances of the electronic information brokering trade will require some adaptation. Promulgating and validating the new values structure will be a fundamental management task which gives cohesion to the procedural changes required.

LIBRARY VERSUS LIBRARY

This is a horrid thought, anathema to our long tradition of cooperative efforts, especially inter-library lending and borrowing. The issue of access vs. ownership, however, brings new stresses to this successful model. Is it possible for the access libraries to become disenfranchised from the knowledge held by the ownership libraries? What are the cost sharing implications, especially for technical services? Do we need now to begin formulation of obligatory agreements ensuring access to all cited materials for the access libraries? How do we divide the archival and preservation responsibilities for materials? Economically, how do we alleviate the collections monies burden on the ownership libraries? Finally, what is the real value of the access dividend from technology? These seem to be a few of the many overarching questions which the profession must address as individual libraries chart their own strategic visions for services and programs. Establishing a balance among libraries with differing missions and values has always been a delicate operation, but this issue may threaten the fundamental cooperative tradition which we prize. We cannot devolve into a "have" and "have not" dichotomy.

A pro-active approach could be initiated through the professional associations and utilities to develop a national information policy for libraries. Such a policy would articulate and identify information resources, obligations for cooperation, delineate responsibilities for contributions, and seek to coordinate the diverse and rich services which libraries offer.

New uses for the North American Collections Inventory Project (NCIP) offer opportunities beyond collections management. How could the tool be used by acquisitions as a knowledge broker? In concert with collections operations, could acquisitions participate more actively in identifying its own collections strengths as a comparative measure to the NCIP? Can the Conspectus become both a directory and a selection tool for acquisition and collections staff? In order to succeed the Conspectus needs higher visibility, innovative programs to expand its use and effectiveness, and it needs firm cooperative agreements for its maintenance. "The Conspectus has now been completed by research libraries across the United States. Using a six-point scale, participants have rated their collections in seven thousand subject categories. Despite its wide adoption, however, the Conspectus has yet to be used to construct a national collection development policy"[4]. . . . The emergence of national networks provides the impetus for us to address real needs with this valuable tool.

APPROACHES AND OPPORTUNITIES

The access/ownership world of libraries is not yet reality. It is clear, however, that this is one of the major issues for library management in a world of tight resources. Harlan Cleveland writes:

. . . the informatization of society does change the context in which these durable dilemmas present themselves in the 1980's and 1990's. Out there in the marketplace of ideas, this expandable, substitutable, transportable, leaky, shareable resource [information] is creating confusion as it undermines our inherited knowledge and wisdom. . . . What is different now is that information is, in all sorts of ways, more accessible than the world's key resources have ever been at any previous time in history. The first task for leaders and potential leaders, then, is to look much more sharply at our heritage of assumptions.[5]

As Walt Kelly's Pogo noted: we are surrounded by insurmountable opportunities. The major opportunity which we must surmount is to become an active participant and molder in the emerging national network. The web of national and international networks represents a remarkable opportunity for acquisitions to re-formulate itself. Use of the network to transfer information, select information, broker information to other outside sources, and to select information sources to serve the access function for our clients can benefit greatly from the acquisitions perspective and function. Current literature and conference programs mention the proposed NREN (National Research and Education Network) frequently. The power of this network to move large stores of data offers an entirely new world for libraries and for acquisitions. Should acquisitions begin the process to recognize remote library catalogs as entries into the local database? What directories and resources exist on the network, and can a library consider those as acquisitions because the library can access them?

A Proposal to Begin

Virgil recommends that we "be favorable to bold beginnings." Given some complex and diverse issues which the new networked environment brings to libraries and our evolving philosophies to focus on access support for our clients, where and how can we begin? Rather than interminable introspection to construct a superstructure to accommodate the full spectrum of the issue, we should focus on an application which has value and targets an audience. From this initial experience, we can learn and apply and adjust as necessary. What is a niche in the communications and knowledge continuum for Libraries and acquisitions?

In "Structuring of the Scholarly Communication System," Charles B. Osburn describes "Outputs and mechanisms of the system":

> The outputs of the scholarly communication system take many forms. They may be published writings, such as books, journal articles, or reports; they may be unpublished writings, such as correspondence, papers, and other memoranda; they may be unrecorded communications in person or vital electronic media of many types. Those communications that most often occur outside the arena of the published or broadly distributed are considered to compose the social phenomenon called the invisible college, which is a highly selective subsystem of scholarly communication.[6]

This description could also apply to the division of responsibilities between the access and ownership libraries. If ownership libraries continued with the traditional acquisition of knowledge in published writings, books, journal articles, etc., then the access libraries in a quid pro quo agreement could focus on the "invisible college" materials, especially those in electronic form. Identification and control of these unpublished communications addresses the issue of archival and records management control historically incumbent upon libraries, and it offers the opportunity to share and expand the knowledge paths of scholarly communication more broadly. Acquisitions should forge stronger liaisons with faculty at the institution, with technology resources on campus, and with compilers of electronic communications systems such as mailing services, bulletin boards, etc. Currently those are materials and information which have no structure for preservation or consistent dissemination. By accepting those responsibilities for each library, as determined by local policy formulation, the library's acquisitions staff address the visibility, isolation, and training issues.

The outcomes of such a direction would maintain an equilibrium between the access and ownership libraries; each would offer resources valuable to the library's mission. A huge and expanding sphere of knowledge would be made more accessible to the academic communities. This presents a new avenue for continued cooperative endeavors between acquisitions and collection development/management operations. The benefit to the service of knowledge to clients is clear: timely information, especially in science and technology, a greater sensitivity to the process of knowledge creation by following the paths of discussion and academic debate, and greater cohesion between the research and instructional missions of institutions.

We are being challenged to adapt and adopt: "Inherent in this protective function of the library—making the system work—is the closely related function of monitoring scholarly communication so that adjustments can be made. No other agent in the system has that function."[7] This discussion offers some ideas for continued discussion and a proposal for scrutiny; perhaps it is a beginning, a point from which to start. But we must start this re-creation of ourselves if we wish to remain a key component in the academic process and structure. A key area to begin this re-creation of ourselves is in acquisitions.

REFERENCES

1. Harlan Cleveland, *The Knowledge Executive: Leadership in an Information Society* (New York, N.Y.: E.P. Dutton, 1985), 29-34.

2. Joe A. Hewitt, "On the Nature of Acquisitions," *Library Resources & Technical Services* 33, no. 2 (1989): 107.

3. Mary Ann Griffin, "Managing Values in an Academic Library," in *Energies for Transition: Proceedings of the Fourth National Conference of the Association of College and Research Libraries, April 9-12, 1986, Baltimore, Maryland* (Chicago, Illinois: Association of College and Research Libraries, 1986), 106.

4. Thomas A. Lucas, "Verifying the Conspectus: Problems and Progress," *College & Research Libraries News* 51, no. 3 (1990): 199.

5. Cleveland, *ibid.*, 34.

6. Charles B. Osburn, "The Structuring of the Scholarly Communication System," *College & Research Libraries* 50, no. 3 (1989), 283.

7. Osburn, *ibid.*, 286.

Budgeting for Users:
Rethinking the Materials Budget

David S. Sullivan

Il n'est pas certain que le melon ait été créé par la divine Providence pour être découpé en tranches. On peut douter si le cochon demande veritablement à être mangé, ou le hareng à mariner, mais les livres, mais les oeuvres humaines, sont conçus pour le plaisir, le regard, le service, et la main de l'homme, bref pour la consommation.

— Dominique Jamet[1]

The agreement is general — if vague — among academic librarians that the collections they form and manage are meant to be used and that all librarians, including those who form research collections, are in the business of providing a service.[2] Despite this agreement, whose expressions range from the abstractions of Buckland to the homier, humaner, and perhaps more helpful observations of Dowd,[3] attempts to resituate the historically central task of libraries, the formation of collections, into the context of service delivery have been few and generally ill-fated. More specifically, there has been little apparent progress in creating frameworks to predict the costs of providing whatever the service is that collections are thought to render. Efforts to budget for academic library acquisitions remain essentially at the stage they were in 1983 (and, I suspect, in 1933), when John Vasi summarized the outcome of a survey of ten research libraries' budgeting practices. He wrote that acquisitions budgets in research libraries were largely based on either historical patterns — proceeding from the appealing notion that it would be

David S. Sullivan is Collection Development Manager and Monograph Acquistions Librarian at Stanford University Libraries.

15

surprising if we weren't already doing the right thing—or on models whose presuppositions were unclear, and whose recommendations were often not followed.[4]

In this paper, I will discuss some of the difficulties raised by the idea of budgeting for users, and propose that perspectives deriving from the idea of the library as a locus of coproduction of knowledge can aid in beginning to design pragmatic approaches to meet these difficulties.

Let me make two detours to set my topic in context.

The first is to point to the state of affairs external to the library that makes more effective allocation of resources for research materials imperative. This context, which has been the object of much discussion in the past three years, is the very steeply rising cost of the materials that researchers are thought to need to conduct their work. Costs are rising for several reasons: the growing concentration of control over scholarly publication in the hands of private organizations who seek to maximize market share and profits; the increasing size of the scholarly—particularly the scientific—community and hence of its literature; adverse trade conditions for purchasers of scholarly information in the United States; and, not least, the determination of many librarians to carry always-expanding, never-contracting serial lists.[5]

If library budgets were as elastic as they were in the 1970's, of course, these conditions might raise issues, but would not constitute a problem. As things stand, however, libraries and their sponsoring organizations find themselves less and less able to maintain acquisitions programs as ambitious as those of past years, and the pinch has now increased in severity to the point that it is no longer feasible to postpone the development of budgeting methods that will allow institutional goals to be stated and met even as the scale of programs is reduced. Put another way, the internal reallocations that have continuously been occurring, but which were hidden by "fat" budgets, are now visible.

The second detour is to examine, very briefly, the kinds of budget models and formulas that currently prevail in academic libraries. This is not done with any intention of deriding the valiant attempts of libraries to budget in an informed way, but to specify how current practice fails to address the needs of library users directly.

Gary Shirk has shown—with more indignation than the subject deserves—that formulas developed so far for allocating materials budgets[6] are (a) not models in the accepted, scientific, sense of the word: they are not explicit expressions of a theory which can be tested against reality; and that (b) even viewed as procedures, what formulas gain in clarity by being stated "mathematically," they lose in credibility because, as he grimly concludes, they cloak ". . . fantasy with the trappings of science."[7]

Shirk's criticism certainly holds true in part for two models with which I am familiar,[8] though I suggest in a later paragraph that the consequences of this are neither as dire, nor quite the same, as he would have them.

The Voigt/Susskind acquisitions model has been employed since the late 1970's by the University of California to project the number of volumes needed by the system each year, and hence as an index for the libraries' budget request to the State. The model proceeds from a base number of volumes per campus (40,000 annually), which is to be augmented by factors representing the presence on each campus of "doctoral programs . . . [and] graduate professional programs with a high degree of independence in their literature," the number of students, and the volume of sponsored research.[9] The model used by the Stanford University Libraries is based on the goal of maintaining constant purchasing power in the world book market, expressed as a steady share of publishing output, and is ascribed by local tradition to the insights of a (conveniently deceased) professor in the Graduate School of Business. Both models are used to drive budget requests that also take into account measured or predicted inflation in the price of library materials. Neither of these models is defensibly based on a theory—or even a description—of what the purpose of collection building is, and neither is comprehensibly related to goals other than the maintenance of a steady internal state of processes within the library.[10]

It is perhaps worth pausing for a moment to reflect that this state of affairs, though it may offend against reason, should scarcely surprise us. Buckland points out that the collection development, as he describes it, accounts for as much as two thirds of total library expenditures in research libraries.[11] Administrators with a need to furnish their sponsoring organizations with accurate predictions of expenses will naturally have a tendency to write budgets in a way that maximizes their ability to attain this accuracy. The obvious way to do this is to base the budget on factors under their own control, and in this way, formulas such as Voigt/Susskind and the Stanford model function essentially as rhetorical devices: by stating their case in terms drawn from the discourses of education, and scholarship ("students," "sponsored research," and so on), they acknowledge their dependence for resources on the values of the parent organization and thereby gain a favorable hearing;[12] the reality behind the rhetoric is the library's internal need to insure that the level of work within the technological core of library operations is stabilized and predictable. This need is met by having the model operate on the simplest units of production within the library, i.e., books and serials, the objects to which librarians do things. So Shirk's complaint, that models cloak ". . . fantasy with the trappings of science," is not quite right. They cloak one perfectly rational strategy, one that aims to meet the internal needs of the library, in the guise of another, that aiming to meet the needs of users. And even if we grant that this strategy clouds the very issues it purports to illuminate, there is no gainsaying the fact that models like Voigt/Susskind have resulted in stable funding levels for the formation of research collections, nor that this stability has probably provided a good context within which research could proceed. As long as there is a lot of material in a library, without obvious discontinuities in coverage, researchers stand some chance of having their needs met.

So much for the external context, and some of the existing approaches to collection budgeting. I now turn to describing what I mean by budgeting for users, how adopting the perspective of co-production can suggest new approaches, to exploring some of the difficulties such approaches would have to surmount to be preferable to current methods, and to proposing some ways to do so.

In this paper, I use the term "budget" to mean the prediction of the financial means necessary to meet programmatic objectives: as Wildavsky puts it, "Budgeting is concerned with the translation of financial resources into human purposes."[13] The most important parts of this definition are that budgets must be predictive; and that they must have an explicitly stated link to programmatic objectives. The core of the case against current budget models is that they state their objectives in terms of variables (material, as it happens) which stand only as proxies for the activities libraries are intended to promote, and that these are not necessarily good proxies for the activities.

I will shortly return to why this is so, but first I need to state more clearly what I mean when I talk of the "use" of the library, the activities it is for. Let me quote George Starr again: ". . . a university library ought to be a space within which writing meets and absorbs the written, thinking finds and appropriates thought."[14] Abstracting for a moment our attention from familiar operational problems, we note that the library is not a box full of books, it is not even a box full of certain books that have been put on shelves in a certain order. It is instead, one of the places where the production of knowledge occurs, and specifically, where the written record of past discoveries is used to create new ones. Unfortunately this sounds rather mystical; unfortunately, it probably is about what happens. What libraries, in their acquisitions budgets (and in the other parts of their budgets that depend on acquisitions) are budgeting *for*, then, is not a level of acquisition of capital assets, but an activity, and, as it happens, an activity performed largely by "partial employees," with outputs that are highly intangible. Obvious as this must sound, it has some consequences which are upsetting to our normal way of doing things, for it means that budgeting, if it is to have the explicit programmatic link that I have called for, has to be aimed at something quite other than assuring that X number of physical volumes (together, these days, with electronic impulses either acquired or "rented") come into building Y in year Z.

And this is where it all gets sticky, on the level of execution; but perhaps helpful in arriving at ways of rethinking budgeting for collections.

First the sticky part. Above I noted that the number of volumes coming into the door (however they may be subdivided or analyzed) are not very good proxies for the adequacy of research collections relative to their cost of acquisition.

Two limit cases may clarify why this is so. Suppose a library acquires nothing in a given field. In that "space within which," it's not unreasonable to think that researchers will not be able to conduct those conversations with the record that Starr asks us to imagine. On the other hand, suppose a library acquires (through some miracle) everything ever published in a given field. Leaving aside the question of information overload, there is no doubt that a researcher in the second library will be in better shape. But, on the other hand, there is no way to determine whether resources have been allocated appropriately, which is the essence of budgeting. Perhaps too many books were bought. Perhaps the same researcher's needs could have been satisfied with half or a quarter the number.[15] And though this is a limit case, and therefore absurd on its face, any budgeting method that is based on the number of books to be acquired (however that may be expressed) is liable to the same criticism. Although it is possible to know that too little has been acquired for people to do their work (because chances are, they will let you know) there is no simple quantitative method that will enable the librarian to answer the university administrator's perennial question: how do you know that you haven't acquired too much? Or, more formally, how do you know that what you have expended on input was appropriate relative to the potential output of new knowledge?—which is, after all, the end justifying the library's existence in the first place.

Measuring the relation between input and output is difficult in all settings in the service sector, but perhaps especially intractable where the activities in question are fairly well isolated from immediate practical concerns,[16] as is usually the case with scholarship. This is certainly not a problem that librarians alone are grappling with, but only a specific instance of the more general problem of estimating the benefits and costs of intellectual activity in general.

The literature on the development of science impact indicators gives suggestive hints on the directions librarians might take in approaching their small version of the larger policy issues involved, but it also underscores the difficulties of assessing the relationship between the input and outputs of knowledge systems. Even though this literature is concerned with the other end, so to speak, of the research process, and specifically with measuring the effectiveness of funding for basic research in terms of the eventual social good that results from it, it is nonetheless of some interest for those, like librarians, who are trying to allocate appropriate sums in order to further the work of researchers. Though this literature has focussed on research in the sciences and technology, I believe its fundamental findings may be extended validly to the research process in general.

In the first place, it now appears that the earlier hope that a naive bibliometrics could provide measurements of the effectiveness of the system of scientific communication[17] has been shaken, and no settled consensus has developed on what to measure, or how to measure it, in order to gauge the effectiveness of, for instance, federal programs in support of basic research.[18] What does seem to have been shown[19] is that simply counting articles in a field is not a particularly good measure of anything (other than the number of articles). This in turn suggests that acquisition budgeting based simply on similar "bean-counting" (for instance, the Stanford budget model, which relates publishing output to a suggested level of acquisition), cannot — by definition — make the connection between academic need and library expenditures which should be the essence of acquisition budgeting. Qualitative criteria need to be developed and applied to do that, and the lesson of scientometrics seems to be that the development of such criteria is heavily discipline-dependent, and must rely on a detailed mental representation of how old knowledge is transformed into new in a given field.[20]

So much for the sticky part: it will, indeed, be difficult to come up with ways to measure and then to evaluate the inputs to the research process. What might be the benefits of undertaking so arduous a task? The answer to this question, I suggest, will be rather in the realm of process than in that of procedure. Let me state two important and general consequences that I think follow from the statement that acquisition budgets should be budgets for use and users.

Perhaps the most important is also the most direct. Budgets and budgeting processes that exclude, either in their conception or in their execution, those most affected by the outcome of the process, are inappropriate.[21] Once it is acknowledged that clients are part of the productive process in which libraries are engaged, it becomes necessary to create what Mills, quoting Weber, refers to as "value-rational" structures to which both the library and its users adhere consciously.[22] Doing otherwise threatens both the organization and its users with the prospect of divergent sets of values coming to the fore when the system is under stress. Even if libraries were able to insulate their concerns from those of their users, they should not, because then the budgeting process is unlikely — at least prima facie — to result in rational allocation of resources. The approach of a library to its sponsoring organization for improvements to its materials budget always has its political aspect; it is my contention that the ensuing process will be more likely to result in appropriate budgeting if such requests are cast explicitly in terms of shared values, and where the competition for resources will be understood in essentially the same way by all parties. This does not happen when budgets for collections are presented in terms such as volume counts that are only indirectly relevant to the research process. For libraries and their clients, the shared value is the worthiness of expending resources to create knowledge, and libraries need to establish ways that will demonstrate a rational and accountable connection between collection building and this value.

Second, budgets aiming to predict the cost of producing intangible outputs from unknown quantities of material input, cannot, at least at the present state of knowledge, be represented by quantitative formulas. The qualitative dimensions of knowledge production are far more important, and the translation of them into quantities (i.e., dollar amounts) is, given our current, very incomplete knowledge of the process, much more likely to be the outcome of expert reflection than of direct calculation.[23] One implication of this for the execution of any plan to budget in the way I am advocating is that the budget process within the library needs to be decentralized, or, rather, re-conceived from the bottom up: in the first place, the programmatic objectives of collection development are established by selectors; in the second, only they have the expert knowledge that makes it possible to arrive at intelligent statements of the contours of their areas of specialization and of the financial resources necessary to meet their objectives.

If all this is granted, one consequence is immediately evident: political processes need to be set in place in which the claims of the various disciplines for support may be weighed against each other. In the foreseeable future, it is unlikely that research libraries will have the luxury of an environment of such abundance that all claims will be fundable; and again, it is crucial, if choices are to be made between programs, that the rival claims are based on clear, shared perceptions of what it is that is being funded.

The role of central library administration then becomes, on the one hand, the creation and maintenance of commonly-needed baseline information. This goes beyond compiling such commonly used statistics as, e.g., numbers of books acquired, book price indexes, amount spent on this or that subject, publishing output by discipline, and must include the development of qualitative tools for evaluating collections in terms of their adequacy to support research. On the other, the center must lead in the creation and management of processes that will be both competitive and enable it to act as an arbiter of equity, so that the internal competition between selectors for funds does not become harmful to the institution's overall goals.

I close with the merest sketch of what this kind of budget process might look like. Under such a model, selectors will be asked to describe in terms of academic program what their collecting goals are for discrete parts of the collection: where are they building research collections, where basic study collections, where is collecting minimal? They will need to be able to describe (and substantiate) in fairly exact, but still qualititative terms, how they know where they are meeting these goals, and where not. I expect they will use the RLG Conspectus as a tool for recording these aims and achievements; but they will also be asked to put price tags on them, and here they will be largely thrown back on their own expertise.

Finally, the pressure of ever-rising materials cost will mean that, in the foreseeable future, there will be more internal competition among selectors for funds than in the past: when goals are associated with budget requests, the latter naturally acquire a political aspect, and this internal competition, if aboveboard and well managed, should give collection development programs a dynamism freeing them from intra-library inertia and making them more directly responsive to the needs of the research community.

NOTES

1. "One can't be certain that the melon was created by divine providence in order to be cut into slices, and one can doubt whether the pig really asks to be eaten, the herring to be marinated. But books, but human creations, are conceived to satisfy our pleasure, our sight, our use, the human hand: in short, in order to be consumed." Editorial in *Réseaux:journal de l'Association des amis de la Bibliothèque de France*, no. 1.

2. This term "use" here has a broad sense: collection developers are notoriously chary of linking their activities with use in the narrower sense of "consultation within a given time period." Schad (1978) p. 329 says, "But even though library materials are acquired for use, use is not the principal goal of academic libraries. That goal is to provide the greatest possible benefit to society. This occurs when members of the academic community bring about the betterment of society . . ." His paper contains a helpful discussion of why book budgeting cannot be based on use-driven models. For in interesting, if somewhat bizarre, approach to allocating book funds that is driven directly by circulation, see Schmitz-Veltin (1984). Among the claimed recommendations of this method is that it "diffused much of the struggle among departments and bibliographers for a larger share of the available funds." (p. 267)

3. Buckland (1989), p. 216, states that the goodness of collections can only be evaluated relative to "a measure of the capability with respect to meeting some definition of intended use" or to "a measure of value . . . which, for collections, implies utilization and beneficial effects." His article is valuable for its clear statement (p. 14f.) of the reasons why collection building is not the same thing as acquiring material, but is akin to cataloging and other forms of file organization, in that its essence is the localization and arrangement of information. Dowd (1989), p. 18, quotes Professor George Starr's definition of what libraries are: " . . . not solely or primarily repositories of information . . . a university library ought to be a space *within* which writing meets and absorbs the written, thinking finds and appropriates the thought. . . . "

4. Vasi (1983) p. 8f. He notes (p. 9) that "The state [California, I presume] using a full formula approach for acquisitions found that its libraries needed about $60,000,000 to catch up to what the formula recommended for . . . acquisitions over the past decade." Schad (1978) gives an overview of formula budgeting since 1931. More recent bibliography concerning acquisitions budgeting is given in Niles (1989).

5. The context is well sketched by Dowd (1989) p. 19, published in an issue of the *Journal of Library Administration* (10:1) devoted entirely to "The Impact of Rising Costs of Serials and Monographs on Library Services and Programs." Unfortunately, the contributions in this volume go little further than to suggest that there is an impact, and that it is significant. The British Library has also made " . . . the implications of information being treated as a tradeable commodity" a priority area of research, see British Library Research and Development Department (1989).

6. Though my paper is on overall acquisition budgeting, in most instances this represents simply the most general case, or the cumulation, of allocations made at lower levels.

7. Shirk (1985), p. 40.

8. And for the models used by research libraries surveyed in an informal poll of budget practices conducted last year as part of Stanford University Libraries' re-examination of our budget model. Most of the libraries surveyed budget, in essence, by requesting inflationary adjustments to support steady-state acquisitions — in other words, simply by assuming that a given level of gross acquisition corresponds to the needs of local researchers.

9. Smith (1984) gives a full description of the model and the history of its development and use.

10. This is true even though Voigt/Susskind is based on variables which purport to measure first, knowledge output, expressed in the factors for fields with independent literatures and for sponsored research, and second, direct use of library materials, expressed in the factors for number of students. These variables are in fact merely labels which are attached to more or less arbitrary constants. That they are arbitrary is perhaps most clearly demonstrated in the fact that the base figure of 40,000 volumes per campus per year has not been adjusted since 1977; in that time, the monographic literature of the developed countries alone has increased by 50%, and the size of the serial literature has probably increased by an ever larger factor. The breakdown of the number of titles by subject (Smith (1984) p. 138), also never revised, has no line for a subject such as computer science, whose literature has increased enormously over the past decade, and does not overlap significantly with that of the parent disciplines from which it arose. If the formula really expressed a hypothesis about the size (and hence cost) of collections needed for research, then this would mean that the claim is being made that the proportion of the literature worth acquiring and preserving is steadily, and fairly rapidly, shrinking. Few academic librarians would advance this claim directly (though it may in fact be true.)

11. Buckland (1989), p. 213. He includes all costs associated with the acquisitions and processing of materials in his calculations.

12. In the terminology of ancient rhetoric, such a strategy is called the "captatio benevolentiae," the seizing of goodwill. Lest I be misunderstood, let me state that I am not suggesting that library officials following this strategy are being disingenuous; only that the consequences of the strategy are such as we might expect.

13. Wildavsky (1968), p. 192.

14. Dowd (1989), p. 18.

15. An aspect of library collections that I am not focussing on, and a quality of academic research are relevant here. The archival function of libraries — though it often looks simply like a random and essentially unmotivated desire to save everything — is of course really predicated on the idea that someone, someday will want to use a given item. On the scholars' side, despite all the research tending to show that past use is the best predictor of future use, and all that showing that the

materials in research libraries are very largely unused, it remains true that it is almost impossible to predict the usefulness of a given title to future researchers, at least in the humanities. And as the humanities extend their interest into areas such as the history of science, even the scientific literature, where such predictions might have fairly high short-term validity, will be called upon increasingly as an archival source.

16. The emphasis here is on "immediate" — obviously scholars' concerns are in many ways as practical as anyone else's, but the time scale within which they are required to be met is different from, say that of a customer of a funeral home or of a fast-food franchise.

17. For instance through more or less straightforward analysis of impact factors as practiced by the Science Citation Index.

18. See the papers of the Augsburg conference on science impact indicators, *Knowledge* v. 9, no. 2, December 1987, edited by William Dunn and Burkart Holzner, especially the papers on the design of science impact indicators (Dunn et al.), the architecture of knowledge systems (Holzner et al.) and the overview of "second generation scientometrics" as a guide to science policy (Chubin).

19. For a representative case study, see Cohn (1986), and Roger Noll's response (Noll (1986)). Cohn develops and tests a model showing that knowledge growth, defined as the location and solution of important problems, is more highly correlated with the progress of subdisciplinary evolution than with funding. A corollary of his study is that there is a good deal of noise in the system of scientific communication, noise, unfortunately, which typically must be acquired by libraries if they are to receive the "signal" as well.

20. A common-sense way of putting this is that libraries need to know how scholars work: easily said, but the difficulty is in building a model that will account both for the wide variation in how people work in different fields, and for the evolution of disciplinary practice.

21. Of course, academic libraries almost always derive the bulk of their funding from their parent organizations, and submit — at least nominally — to their imperatives. But budget requests that are driven by, or expressed in terms of, the libraries' internal processes, are the rule rather than the exception.

22. Mills (1986), Chapter 5 passim, but see especially pp. 79-82. Mills' concern is mostly to show how subjective, but rational, structures, control service-providers' activities, but, in his more general formulation — ". . . values serve both to discriminate among possible courses of action and to rationalize individual behavior or actions that are taken." (p. 81) — the notion applies to behaviors such as budgeting and other institutional priority-setting.

23. In a recent discussion at Stanford, one selector worried that reliance on such expert opinion would lead to a subjective allocation of funds, since it was being proposed, as he thought, to do away with "objective correlates" for budget decisions. Another selector remarked that there was an objective correlate, namely the selector's salary.

REFERENCES

Bentley and Farrell (1984). Stella Bentley and David Farrell, Beyond retrenchment: the reallocation of a library materials budget. *Journal of Academic Librarianship* v. 10, no. 6, pp. 321-325.

British Library Research and Development Department (1989). Priorities for research 1989-1994. *International Journal of Information and Library Research* v. 1, no. 1.

Buckland (1989). Michael K. Buckland, The roles of collections and the scope of collection development. *Journal of Documentation* v. 45, no. 3, September 1989, pp. 213-226.

Cohn (1986). Steven F. Cohn, The effects of funding changes on the rate of knowledge growth in algebraic and differential topology. *Social Studies of Science*, v. 16, pp. 23-59.

Dowd (1989). Sheila T. Dowd, Fee, fie, foe, fum: will the serials giant eat us? *Journal of Library Administration* v. 10, no. 1, pp.17-38.

Mills (1986). Peter K. Mills, Managing service industries: organizational practices in a postindustrial economy. Cambridge, MA: Ballinger, 1986.

Niles (1989). Judith Niles, The politics of budget allocation. *Library Acquisitions: Theory and Practice*, v. 13, pp. 51-55.

Noll (1986). Roger Noll, Discussants' comments. *Social Studies of Science*, v. 16, pp. 135-50.

Schad (1978). Jasper G. Schad, Allocating materials budgets in institutions of higher education. *Journal of Academic Librarianship*, v. 3, no. 6, 1978, pp. 328-332.

Schmitz-Veltin (1984). Gerhard Schmitz-Veltin, Literature use as a measure for funds allocation. *Library Acquisitions: Practice and Theory* (8), 1984, pp. 267-274.

Shirk (1985). Gary M. Shirk, Allocation formulas for budgeting library materials: science or procedure? *Collection Management* v. 6, nos. 3/4, Fall/Winter 1984, pp. 37-43.

Vasi (1983). John Vasi, Budget allocation systems for research libraries. (OMS Occasional paper, 7). Washington: ARL, 1983.

Wildavsky (1968). Aaron Wildavsky, Budgeting as a political process, in David L. Sills, ed. *The international encyclopedia of the social sciences* 2:192-199.

Threats and Opportunities: Collection Development in a Changing Research Library Environment

Connie Kearns McCarthy

SUMMARY. How does the organizational climate of today's research library affect collection development? How is the climate of the library affected by the larger institutional climate? What is the impact on collection development and the role of the bibliographer?

The article looks at general management theory on change and applies that theory to the role of the bibliographer in a changing environment. The bibliographer is viewed as an important contributor in defining organizational goals. The bibliographer, as any library manager, has the skills and perception to navigate the "permanent white water" in coping with change.

INTRODUCTION

Glance at any recent library conference program and you can identify several sessions which deal with topics such as "Changing Research Libraries," "Managing Changing Information Needs," "Managing the Information Explosion." What is this "changing research library?" How well are we managing this changing environment? And how does all this change particularly affect collection development in our research libraries?

Rosabeth Moss Kanter has a definition of change that is particularly applicable to today's research library: "Change involves the crystallization of new action possibilities (new policies, new behaviors, new patterns, new methodologies, new products, or new mar-

Connie Kearns McCarthy is Assistant University Librarian, Perkins Library, Duke University, Durham, NC 27706.

ket ideas) based on reconceptualized patterns in the organization. The architecture of change involves the design and construction of new patterns, or the reconceptualization of old ones, to make new, and hopefully more productive, actions possible." (1:279)

It is critical that we be able to reconceptualize the possibilities for the future of research libraries. To do so, we must examine the organizational climate of the library within the broader context of the university. The climate of the library is, of course, reflective of the parent organization.

CLIMATE OF HIGHER EDUCATION

Major research institutions are facing lean economic times and are beginning to look to managing their institutions with the same businesslike approach as their corporate counterparts. A recent article in the *Chronicle of Higher Education* spoke of Columbia University's philosophy of "selective excellence" as the institution attempts to bring rising costs under control. The article identifies the reality of higher education today: "many of the nation's most prestigious private research universities now find their budgets pinched uncomfortably between skyrocketing costs and increasing resentment over the high tuitions they charge. They . . . are engaged in cutting back administrative and academic programs in order to polish their overall educational quality." (1:A1, A31)

CLIMATE OF RESEARCH LIBRARIES

In many ways, the research library as a major business within the university has been facing skyrocketing costs for several years. While all costs generally increase, probably the cost that has most directly influenced our strategies of collection development has been the rising cost in serial publications. In addition, our acquisitions budgets face increasing demand for the purchase of multiple formats of materials, as we introduce new products in CD-ROM and databases.

In similar ways, the research libraries have had to look to ways to "polish their overall educational quality." In the case of libraries, this has meant evaluating the overall cost-effectiveness of the organization. In many ways, new technology has enabled the library to streamline procedures for technical operations and to make qualitative and economic gains. However, we need to pick up our pace and reach maximum productivity to avoid dangerous cutbacks that may be necessary at the university level.

COLLECTION BUILDING IN THE CURRENT CLIMATE

To gain this same level of "productivity" in terms of our collection building is not so easy. However, the collection development program does need to be in tune with the general university program. If the institution eliminates, or de-emphasizes a program, what is the effect on the library collections? How will the materials budget be adjusted to reflect those changes? Does the library have strong, historical collections in the area being de-emphasized? Is the historical collection of such value that its support should be continued? Do the collections provide support for resource sharing partners that will be affected? These are questions that need to be raised with faculty and administrators as program evaluations are made.

We have all had experiences when new programs are initiated and faculty in new research fields are brought to the institution with expectations that library resources are adequate or will be expanded to meet new program needs. All too frequently, new funds for library resources have not been identified. It is equally important for the bibliographer to identify inadequate resources. Assuming that the "library will provide" without establishing new resources puts a serious strain on other subject areas and serves to weaken the overall quality of the collections.

Building and shaping a collection requires that bibliographers be responsive to the changing needs of the clientele, that they be able to anticipate future research needs of scholars, as well as to respond to current teaching and research needs. Bibliographers in touch with the clientele are in a unique position as collection managers to be "change masters." Kanter's term is appropriate: "those people and organizations adept at the art of anticipating the need for, and of leading, productive change." (1:13)

In examining how bibliographers might play the role of change masters, my model of the bibliographer is that of the dual role bibliographer—a branch librarian or reference librarian/bibliographer. These libraries are particularly well poised to view the changing demands of the clientele, as well as to view the changes in the delivery and availability of information.

"Permanent White Water"

As collection managers are coping with change, bibliographers are subject to the same external and internal forces as are other library managers. A particularly apt metaphor might be that of "permanent white water," which Peter Vaill used in *Managing as a Performing Art: New Ideas for a World of Chaotic Change.* The sensation as he describes it is that of not being able to paddle on calm waters and not being able to get out of the rapids. "No sooner do you begin to digest one change that another one comes along to keeps things unstuck. In fact, there are usually lots of changes going on at once. The feeling is one of continuous upset and chaos." (3:2)

While the continuous changes in our libraries may bring the feeling of "continuous upset and chaos," we know that many navigate difficult and treacherous white water, and those that do well have acquired the skills, knowledge and flexibility to pursue the adventure with enthusiasm and excitement.

Organizational Values

As we evaluate the organizational climate, which we tend to do in evaluating any change, we seek to establish values that frame our approach. In accepting the change, Vaill suggests we look at five frontiers of organizational values; economic, technological, communal, sociopolitical, and transcendental. It might be helpful to evaluate these "frontiers" in the context of libraries and library collection development.

Economic Values

In managing the business of the library, whether it be the collections budget or the total library budget, our fiscal decisions are, in effect, value judgments on our priorities. What is it we really need to provide? Do we gain efficiencies in selected budget lines to strengthen our provision of strong services or collections?

Technological Values

Technological changes are not new to libraries. Our past developments in online cataloging, online catalogs and delivery of information have brought changes in technology. The values that we now need to continue to evaluate are issues of productivity and efficiency. In evaluating materials for the collections, we increasingly need to continue to evaluate are issues of productivity and efficiency. In evaluating materials for the collections, we increasingly need to assess issues of access to collections in various formats as well as to examine a variety of new methods of delivery of materials.

Communal Values

The communal value addresses the needs of the employees. What kind of a community does the organization, the library, want to be? What are the values in being associated with this particular organization?

Sociopolitical Values

The library is often perceived as the "heart of the institution." It is vital to the institution. As with any other department or activity on campus, the library seeks to define its relationships to its constituencies. The bibliographer, as a key link to faculty and faculty departments, communicates the vitality of the library to its users and at the same time is able to identify user issues to library administrators.

Transcendental Values

The mission or purpose of the organization is important to those within and without. It is important that the bibliographers play a role in defining that mission. It is also essential to the library's mission that the bibliographers partake of this vision and become effective communicators to those outside the institution with whom they come in contact.

IMPACT ON BIBLIOGRAPHER

What is the impact of the managerial theory on change on the individual bibliographer and the consequent impact on collection development? Bibliographers as collection managers can and do play a key role in helping to define organizational values. Library administrators need to recognize the role of change master for the bibliographer. Bibliographers are critical contributors in the process of navigating those turbulent waters. They need to use their skills and perception to help define institutional values. They must struggle with increased burdens on the collection budget as well as changes in the delivery of information. Technological changes and economic demands make the decision-making tasks increasingly more difficult.

Bibliographers will face added responsibilities. They will need to continue to shape collections in traditional ways; print collections will remain. What is added is the evaluation and decision process required to provide new and alternative means of both determining and access to their collections.

REFERENCES

1. Grassmuck, K. "Columbia U. Uses Philosophy of 'Selective Excellence' to make Painful Cuts in Programs, Administration." *The Chronicle of Higher Education* 36(32) (April 25, 1990): A1, A31.

2. Kanter, R.M. *The Change Masters*. New York: Simon and Schuster, 1983.

3. Vaill, P.B. *Managing as a Performing Art: New Ideas for a World of Chaotic Change*. San Francisco, Jossey-Bass, 1989.

Collection Development
for the Nineties:
A Context for Evaluation

John F. Riddick

SUMMARY. As the decade begins, collection development faces the burgeoning number of book and serial publications within a framework of diminished national and state resources provided to higher education. Without a sharply compelling force such as depression, war or revolution, libraries will likely continue to agonize over this conflict as the decade unfolds. Slowly the traditional ownership of journals will be exchanged for access to them through CD-ROM or other full text retrieval methods. The latter scenario will offer improved access at similar, if not higher, charges. Juxtaposed to this transition will be the search for clearer answers as to library materials use studies and the political consequence of their use. The picture of access, ownership and pricing will likely remain unclear unless the Federal Government attempts to impose greater regulation and control over the flow of information.

INTRODUCTION

Collection development is a shambles. As a pristine tidy management concept, development of the nation's library collections has been whipsawed into near meaninglessness by inflation, questionable price increases, currency exchange variations, diminished support of higher education, and an ever increasing abundance of publishable research. Most academic library budgets pay increasing

---

John F. Riddick is Associate Professor and Head of the Acquisition Services Department, Charles V. Park Library, Central Michigan University, 204 Park Library, Mt. Pleasant, MI 48858.

He holds a BA and an MA in history from Western Michigan University and an AMLS from the University of Michigan.

homage to serials, especially scientific serials, to the neglect of book purchases and the social sciences and humanities. Common belief implies that collection development is a thoughtful proactive long term plan for the gathering of library publications. What bosh! The execution of collection development for the bulk of today's university libraries could be likened to the desperate search of an Ethiopian woman for food and drink to sustain her ebbing babe's life.

CAUSES OF CHAOS

How did collection development arrive at this state? Well, certainly Cheever, the butler, did not do it. First, a world wide sweep of economic greed associated with the political economic philosophy of Ronald Reagan, Margaret Thatcher, Helmut Kohl, and Yasuhiro Nakasone established an environment in which each player in the information game could seek the maximum possible personal gain. Consequently, the social programs which included bountiful funds for higher education fell before the chant of "no new taxes." Deregulation prevailed throughout the Western-styled economies. New international publishing combines faced few restraints to their inflationary cost increases and demanded allegedly "a little more" as their charges for books and especially serials grew. With an increased number of volumes and pages, the publisher likewise responded to the needs of university faculty members seeking publication for tenure, promotion, or love of research. The library could, for awhile, allow the increasing number of costly journals to erode book purchases to the level of 60% or 70% of the entire acquisitions budget. Somewhere in that range of journal spending, the dogs of war were unleashed by library directors as serials cancellation programs brought howls of pain and anguish from affronted faculty. Thus everyone has lost. The publisher's print runs of books and serials have diminished. While maintaining what would appear to be substantial profit levels, highly respected publishers have fallen in perception to the level of voracious capitalist dogs. The brilliance of academe has perceptibly faded with the tarnish emanating from the crass theme of publish or perish. Meanwhile, the faculty member's bleating appears ungoverned, unrealistic and self-serving. Finally, the micawber-like librarian remains in a posture of hoping that "something will turn up."

Although most of the knowledge-based players have "lost " in varying degrees, the most key member of the information chain, the knowledge user, possesses the promise of doing rather well, mostly through the use of presently available and forthcoming automation and/or computer associated products. These are the forces which will drive the themes of collection development through the nineties as automated access to information plays an increasingly significant role in the flow of research from publisher to user.

MORE KNOWLEDGE, NEW ANSWERS?

The increasing flow of information will continue throughout the nineties. Although some "naysayers" will attempt to tie this academic production to the forces of publish or perish, this accusation misses the mark by a wide margin. Yes, certainly, some publication emanates from the system of academic rewards. I contend, however, that a great deal more publication of very high quality comes from well grounded scholars who research and write out of pride, competitive urge, love of the subject and the process of research. The single truth which outweighs all the above tendencies, however, is the essential freedom of expression found in Western Civilization. It can be guaranteed that as this freedom spreads throughout Eastern Europe, the Soviet Union and, someday, the People's Republic of China, the quality and quantity of publications will grow in size and enrichment as never before experienced.

How can collection development librarians respond to this new explosion of information in what might be considered as a new renaissance? How could a collection development policy be developed to cope with such a challenging scenario? It should be obvious by this time that the traditional concept of ownership simply will not work. The emerging theme of the nineties must be access, initially along the lines suggested by Becky Lenzini as represented in her vision of periodicals unbound, with faxed access to specifically needed articles.[1] In consequence, larger numbers of acquisition dollars will be devoted to automation, line charges, and rapidly improving fax equipment or those items of equipment which mean offering rapid and quality access to the body of journal literature. A core of print-on-paper journals and books will continue to be received in each academic library center, but their purchase will be tied to use studies measuring demonstrable need, not prejudice, whimsy and political clout of library staff or faculty. New and certain methods of data collection will be necessary here to validate the decisions regarding ownership over access.[2]

Will periodicals unbound, faxed article delivery, CD-ROM full text mean more money for books in collection development plans? No. In all likelihood traditional standing order dollars and more will be simply rechanneled to buy computer equipment and to fund access charges to numerous data bases. Book prices will continue upward and will occupy a smaller and smaller part of the acquisition dollars. Smaller print runs will be made by publishers, subject bibliographers will make increasingly critical purchase decisions, and interlibrary loan will have to serve the remainder.

Here, purchases decisions will increasingly be driven by collection evaluation studies rooted in use studies emanating from data collected by automated circulation systems. The certainty of "I think" will no longer work as a point of decision for a book's purchase. "I know" must be the driving force of the decision to purchase tied to a high level of probability focused in empirical evidence. As prudent, wise, and responsible as this might be, how boring would be such a collection development policy rooted in scientific method rather than the flowing art of intellectual impulse.

In recent years, interest in resource sharing and collaborative purchasing has been principally directed to the subject of serial standing orders. These efforts have failed to gain notable wide success.

Perhaps we will find as we pass through the forthcoming decade greater collaboration in collection development will occur in the purchase of monographs. Why not? We have for years operated an effective automated interlibrary loan process within a fairly precise set of protocols. With the sense of how precisely certain vendors' approval plans operate, might it not be possible, within natural groupings of cooperative libraries, to buy books according to these decision patterns which, in reality, could be considered a segment of a collection development plan applied over several libraries? This theme would parallel the intent of the RLG Conspectus but would imply perhaps a greater pre-purchase framework for acquisition decisions.

The major new concept in academic funding for libraries will realize the long held concept of Dr. Richard Rowe that information is not free. In consequence, students might pay a specific fee similar to that of tuition or board and room but this time for library materials and services. The closest existing parallel to this practice is at Western Michigan University where a $50.00 fee is collected each semester from each student to support the purchase of, in part, their integrated library system. In some cases these monies could supplement state appropriated or regularly provided funds while at other institutions they might form the total basis of the library's acquisition and information services budget. In this scenario the faculty member would be charged a proportionately higher fee for presumably greater use of the library. What greater irony than to have the "demon" producer of all this research help pay for its entry into the local information system.

AUTOMATION

CD-ROM will continue to deepen its impact on collection development in the nineties. How many students do you see using *Readers' Guide* compared to *Infotrak* or *Psychlit* matched to the use of *Psy Abstracts*. On a use basis, the CD-ROM indexes have blown the printed indexes out of the water. Necessarily more dollars will be required to fund these and other new indexes. A double twist exists here. University administrators are suckers for the purchase of automation. CD-ROM smacks of being progressive, it possesses a shiny, whiz bang attraction and it avoids the pitfall of throwing more money at the tired, tattered, traditional print-on-paper product. Thus, monies for the micro computer, CD-ROM player, printer, and first year's subscription to the disks are readily funded in a neat package from university equipment funds. In the second and succeeding years, however, collection development funding must find the resources to absorb the disk subscription. To frost the cake, a number of CD-ROM purchasers price the CD-ROM product in such a manner that a continued subscription to the print index cannot be avoided.

Close on the heels of the CD-ROM index is the CD-ROM product providing full text of journal titles. Presently University Microfilms International offers *Business Periodicals Ondisc* consisting of over 300 titles covering about two years of business and management journal articles.

The future of this medium as a source of complete text is full of promise. A single 5 1/2 inch quadruple density disk can store 2.5 million pages of text or when positioned in a juke-box of perhaps four discs would be capable of holding ten million pages of text.[4]

GIFT AND EXCHANGE – A CHARADE?

Gift and Exchange programs may shrink some as the nineties unfold. The great serial exchange programs such as the one established by Charles Harvey Brown at Iowa State University with the nations behind the Iron Curtain will continue at least as long as foreign currency regulations preclude direct sale or purchase. Gift subscriptions of business house organs, religious magazines, and other peripheral types will maintain their inconsequential presence in the collection.

Gift book collections will continue to be coyly solicited in collection development policies and will just as certainly continue to be the bane of acquisitions staff. Oh, so rarely does a gem turn up in that damp smelly box, long the occupant of someone's garage or cellar. And what of the crass dictum that those who give their books to the library will later give their wealth? Nonsense! Maybe this is true at Princeton or Stanford, but for the bulk of "Middle State Universities for the Poor" – forget it.

Do you know anyone who uses the Russian language Proceedings of the Annual Animal Breeding Conference at the University of Kiev? How many agriculture faculty or graduate students are going to seriously examine this serial? In the nineties, such titles obtained on exchange will form the fundamental numerical significance of America's great research libraries. Maybe this is why the University of Michigan's Richard Dougherty refused to submit collection holdings statistics. Was he being perverse or a realist?

COLLECTION DEVELOPMENT AND LITERACY

Americans do not read any more, or, at least, they do it very badly, and collection development policies will have to respond to this trend. Unless the plug is pulled on the television, computer terminal or video game, the love and ability to read will continue to pass into history for many students, and no amount of bemoaning of this fact by Alan Bloom and Page Smith will stop it.[5,6] Paralleling this trend is the continued lowering of admission standards by university admissions offices fighting for the diminished number of apple-cheeked eighteen-year-old youngsters. Or, as this pool dries up, the gathering up of adults who missed college the first time around progresses. If this state of illiteracy is an arguable premise, why fight the issue? If these kids are of the electronic generation then educate them electronically with audio CD's, videos, interactive video learning packages, etc. Thus, why should a collection development policy not include the purchase of these materials? Do we really care if a junior history student learns about the Siege of Khe Sanh from a book or a starkly grim video?

THE COLLECTION DEVELOPMENT MANAGER

What characteristics will be associated with the collection development manager in the nineties? As in previous decades the manager will exercise planning, policy making, preservation application, user liaison, resource sharing, program evaluation and fiscal management. A number of new characteristics will additionally emerge. A general knowledge of automation will likely predominate. It will include manipulating collection use data, fiscal information, and other records in order to make reasonably informed evaluations on collection purchases. A second area of change focuses on academe's growing number of interdisciplinary offerings in both the sciences and social sciences. Third, as the importance of the Pacific Rim emerges and with the opening societies of Eastern Europe and the Soviet Union, new knowledge bases will be required to select quality publications from these areas, particularly in the humanities and social sciences.

As the decade passes, the collection development manager's role may likely change from building collections to adding services as suggested earlier. The manager in liaison with public service staff may emphasize not what the local collection has, but to what publications the library has access. Although the scholar bookman will not disappear from collection development circles, the portfolio of duties will certainly broaden as the century closes.

GOVERNMENT REGULATION?

In the nineties and for awhile thereafter, collection development will continue to face the crunch of rising materials charges. As the nation slowly moves from an economy essentially based in consumer goods to one focused on the knowledge industries, much greater political attention will be directed to the processes and costs of producing and distributing information. Even now, small beginnings are being made. For example, two years ago the European Economic Commission began a fact finding investigation of allegedly discriminatory pricing structures by British publishers within the Community. In America, a number of national library organizations are attempting to galvanize Congressional hearings, or at least raise interest in the problems of information distribution. Any possible legislation, rulings or regulation of the information chain, if appropriate and possible, will likely be many years away.

CONCLUSION

As the nineties unfold, a divergence will emerge among America's academic libraries. Those of the size and complexity associated with the Association of Research Libraries will attempt to continue to build library collections in both great breadth and depth. The pleasant collaborative encouragements of the RLG Conspectus will cut as little ice with the university administration as a record of good sportsmanship but a losing season for the football team. Pride and tradition will likely insulate these three dozen "great" libraries from the possible "wild" visions rendered earlier in this paper. For the several thousand libraries associated with the new state universities, colleges, junior colleges, and especially special libraries (law, business, and medicine) we will see by utter necessity wide sweep-

ing changes in collection development principles which will set the
pace as we enter the twenty-first century.

NOTES

1. Rebecca Lenzini, *"Articles Unbound: Classical Comments on Journals: Presentation Made at Charleston Conference on Issues in Book and Serial Acquisition."* November 4, 1988.
2. Barbara Moran, *Academic Libraries: The Changing Knowledge Centers of Colleges and Universities.* Washington, D.C.: Association for the Study of Higher Education, 1984. p. 75.
3. University Microfilms International. "Business Periodicals Ondisc Product Description," 1989. p. 40.
4. Richard Rowe, *The Economics of Scholarly Communication.* Library Acquisitions: Practice & Theory, Vol. 13., pp. 423-427, 1989.
5. Alan Bloom, *The Closing of the American Mind,* (New York: Simon and Schuster, 1987).
6. Page Smith, *Killing the Spirit,* (New York: Viking, 1989).

REFERENCE

Anthony W. Ferguson, Joan Grant and Joel S. Rutstein, "The RLG Conspectus," *College and Research Libraries*, 49 (May 1988): 197-206.

EVALUATING COLLECTIONS

Translating the Conspectus: Presenting Collection Evaluation Results to Administrators

Jane Treadwell
Charles Spornick

SUMMARY. The RLG Conspectus, although originally developed as a vehicle for cooperative collection development, may have its greatest utility at the local level for describing collections and for fashioning collection development policy statements. Even for this use, the Conspectus presents difficulties. With its codes for describing collection levels and the seemingly subjective determination of those levels, the results from the Conspectus may be unintelligible to university administrators. What is required is a translation of Conspectus findings into a language more readily understood by administrators. At Emory University, findings from Conspectus worksheets and narratives were translated into bar graph charts, allowing for a visual presentation of current and desired collecting levels. The charts were representative, including only selected lines from work-

Jane Treadwell is Director of Collection Management and Charles Spornick is Coordinator for History & Humanities at the Robert W. Woodruff Library, Emory University, Atlanta, GA 30322.

sheets. The result was an executive summary of less than fifty pages created from more than a thousand pages of worksheets and text.

INTRODUCTION AND LITERATURE REVIEW

The RLG Conspectus, developed by the Research Libraries Group as a vehicle for cooperative collection development,[1] has been widely adopted as a tool for collection evaluation. The North American Collections Inventory Project (NCIP) uses the Conspectus as its basis[2] and the LIRN project in the Pacific Northwest has adapted the Conspectus methodology for the use of small and medium-sized libraries as well as large research libraries.[3] Various other regional consortia also have used the Conspectus or some adaptation of it as the basis for cooperative collection evaluation projects.

Like RLG, most groups who have used the Conspectus have had as a goal cooperative, coordinated collection development. However, it now seems that the Conspectus has the greatest utility at the local level, for describing individual collections and serving as the basis for collection development policy statements. Ferguson et al., have identified a number of internal uses of the Conspectus, including determining collecting priorities, improving faculty-library communication, and fundraising.[4] The Conspectus is not, however, without its detractors. Henige, for instance, writes that the Conspectus is too imprecise and subjective to justify belief in its results, and proposes the National Shelf-List Count as a better way to measure collection strength.[5]

Even for those who are convinced that the Conspectus represents an effective collection evaluation methodology, it can still present difficulties. With its codes for describing collecting levels and the seemingly subjective determination of those levels, the Conspectus may be inaccessible to faculty and to library and university administrators. Furthermore, administrators may believe that the Conspectus does not serve as a practical guide for determining budget allocations. Collection development librarians, familiar with the "language of the levels,"[6] need to translate the information gained from a collection evaluation using the Conspectus into a language that is more readily understood by administrators.

THE LANGUAGE OF THE CONSPECTUS

Atkinson speaks of the collection development policy as a system of specialized signs, and maintains that "the key to making, writing, and using collection policy is to understand how its constituent elements interrelate."[7] He proposes a theoretical construct, which if fully understood by the selector, should allow movement from the current to the desired state of the collection.

Collection development policy, as formulated by the Conspectus, assigns a number for the existing collection strength that is arrived at by comparing one's own collection to an ideal collection in the subject. While the assessment process offers many helpful quantitative measures that can aid in deciding on this matter, ultimately the selector must use his or her judgment in assigning a value to the collection. Once the existing collection strength has been agreed upon, the other numbers, for current and desired collecting intensity, then follow according to factors quite often dependent upon the institutional environment, both within the library and in the larger universe of the campus.

When it comes time to write a policy that will be distributed to the wider campus community of faculty and administrators, the numerical language of the Conspectus is usually translated into terms that describe the levels in terms of academic utility: basis, study, research, comprehensive.[8] Still the reader of the policy is left with ECS, CCI, and DCI (Existing Collection Strength, Current Collecting Intensity, Desired Collecting Intensity) for which definitions and distinctions must always be kept in mind. Even if these are spelled out, and not left encoded, there remains the troubling question, how do we get from here (current collection strength) to there (desired collecting intensity)? Atkinson says the collection development policy "should permit the selector to infer how to transform the collection from the current to the desired state."[9] But if the selector, who after all played a major part in assigning the current and desired levels, must somehow infer how to arrive at the desired level, then how much greater must be the perplexity of the library or university administrator, who must make available to the selector the funds necessary for reaching the desired level.

For the selector, the problem of getting from x (existing collecting strength) to z (desired collecting intensity)[10] is, to oversimplify, a matter of identifying what and how much to select. For the administrator, it is a matter of knowing how much it will cost, not only in terms of materials funds, but also in terms of human effort. Thus, the CCI (Current Collecting Intensity) contains more information than the number alone would suggest. While the ECS and the DCI are essentially static, the CCI is active, causing the movement on the scale between the other two numbers.

Another problem for the administrator in dealing with Conspectus results (i.e., the completed collection development policy statement) is one of sheer volume. Most collection development policy statements from large research libraries fill one or more large ring binders. The Conspectus in its entirety has over 7,000 subject descriptors (commonly referred to as lines), not all of which have the same weight, either within or among subjects. For resource-sharing on a national level this amount of detail is appropriate. For assigning priorities on a local level, however, those parts of the Conspectus that most nearly reflect the local academic scene must somehow be highlighted.

TRANSLATION AT EMORY

What follows is an account of how one university library translated its Conspectus findings for the use of administrators. Emory University joined the Research Libraries Group in 1985. Soon after, the Collection Management Division was given a directive to carry out an assessment of the entire General Libraries collections, and to report the findings to the University administration.[11] By virtue of RLG membership, Emory was committed to using the Conspectus as its assessment methodology. The Conspectus also turned out to be very adaptable to internal needs.

As the assessment project progressed, it was decided that to simply present university administrators with the Conspectus results as they were sent to RLG would be ineffective. The sheer length of the document, coupled with the number of lines which were not particularly relevant for Emory, argued against this approach. A narrative synopsis was considered, but it, too, was ruled out because it would have lacked impact. The collection was inadequate in many areas, but how many times could we say that a subject needed to move from a teaching to a research level without losing the reader's interest?

Finally it was decided to create an executive summary in bar graph form to present to the Administration. The existing collection strength and the desired collecting intensity could be represented by different symbols on the graph, the DCI picking up where the ECS ended. In addition to the Conspectus numbers 0-5, the words to describe each level were used also. For example, the graph for African History outlined two areas requiring development from the teaching level to the research level, two areas that were adequately served at the teaching level and so forth (see Figure 1). The CCI or current collecting intensity could not be represented in this linear fashion unless it has been done in the form of an overlay, which could have been confusing. Instead, it was conveyed to a certain extent in the cost summary at the end of each bar graph chart. The cost summary was divided into three parts: the increase (to the base budget) required for books and serials, and the amount needed for retrospective purchases. The third element of each summary statement, which preceded the other two, was a brief profile of the primary department which the collection served. This profile listed only the highest degree offered, the number of faculty, and the number and level (undergraduate, graduate) of students.

The focal point of each summary was, of course, the bar graph chart. For most subjects, all Conspectus lines could be included on a chart of one or two pages. If a subject could not be accommodated on two pages, in many cases the lines were reduced. Lines were sometimes eliminated for subdivisions, or for aspects of the subject that were less significant at Emory. Such a reduction can be seen by comparing the summary chart of African history (Figure 1) with the beginning of the Conspectus worksheet for this area (Figure 2).

FIGURE 1. History—Africa

DEGREES OFFERED: B.A., M.A
FACULTY: 2 (including 1 ILA appt.)
STUDENTS: Undergraduate: 18   Graduate: 3 (no majors)

EXISTING AND DESIRED COLLECTION LEVELS: Existing: ******   Desired: >>>>>>

SUBJECT	NONE 0	MINIMAL 1	BASIC 2	TEACHING 3	RESEARCH 4	COMPRE-HENSIVE 5
Periodicals & General Wrks.	**********************>>>>>>>>>					
History, General	**********************>>>>>>>>>					
Egypt	**********************>>>>>>>>>					
Sudan	**********************					
No. Africa	*********>>>>>>					
No. Africa - 19th-20th C.	**********					
Libya	******************>>>>>>>>>>					
Tunisia	******************					
Algeria	********************************					
Morocco	********************************					
Western Sahara	*********>>>>>>					
West Africa	****************>>>>>>>>>>>>>>>					
W. Africa - Anglophone	***************>>>>>>>>					

Nigeria   *********************************>>>>>>>>>>>>>
W. Africa - Francophone *********************>>>>>>>>>>>>>>>>>
East Africa   *******************>>>>>>>>>>>>>>>>>>>>>
Kenya   *************>>>>>>>>>>>>>>>>>>>>>>>>
Uganda   ***********>>>>>>>>>>>>>>>>>>>>>>>>>
Tanzania   ***********>>>>>>>>>>>>>>>>>>>>>>>>>
Central Africa   *********>>>>>>>>>>>>>
Southern Africa   ***********>>>>>>>>>>>>>>>>>>>>>>
South Africa   *********************************>>>>>>>>>>>>

The development of the collection to the Research Level (4) for Anglophone and
Francophone West Africa, selected areas of East Africa (Kenya, Uganda, and
Tanzania), and Southern Africa would require: the acquisition of an additional
210 titles per year, totalling $5,250 (@ $25 per title); the subscription to an
additional thirty (30) journal titles, totalling $900 (@ $30 per title); and a
one-time allocation of $90,000 for the purchase of retrospective materials
(3,000 titles @ $30 per title).

TOTALS: ANNUAL INCREASE: Books $ 5,250
                          Serials $ 900
                 RETROSPECTIVE PURCHASES: $ 90,000

FIGURE 2

APPENDIX I - HISTORY RLG CONSPECTUS-EMORY UNIVERSITY GENERAL LIBRARIES

LC CLASS		SUBJECT GROUP	ECS	CCI	DCI	COMMENTS
	AFRICA					
DT1-14	NONRLG	Periodicals, General Works	2E	2E	3F	ECS: High 2; the development of graduate programs in African Studies will require 4 level collections for specific regions & periods.
DT15-16	HIS461	Ethnography	1E	1E	1E	
DT17-30	NONRLG	History, General	2E	2E	3E	
DT31-38	HIS462	Political & Diplomatic History	2E	2E	3E	
	HIS463	Colonies & Possessions	2E	2E	3E	
DT	HIS463.10	Colonies & Possessions-British	3E	3E	3E	Low 3
DT	HIS463.20	Colonies & Possessions-French	2F	2F	2F	
DT	HIS463.30	Colonies & Possessions-Portuguese	1E	0	1E	
DT43-107	HIS464	Egypt	2E	2E	3F	High 2. Antiquities

and Modern Period=3

LC	Course	Description				Notes
DT57-69,73	HIS465	Egypt-Antiquities, Egyptology	3F	3F	3F	
DT83-93	HIS466	Egypt-Ancient & Early to 638 A.D.	2F	2F	3F	
DT95-98	HIS467	Egypt-Moslems, 638-1798	1F	1F	3F	
DT100-107	HIS468	Egypt-Nineteenth and Twentieth Centuries, to 1952	2F	2F	2F	French language material
DT107	HIS469	Egypt-1952 to Present	3F	3F	3F	Arabic language material
DT	HIS470	Egypt-Local History & Description	2F	2F	2F	Based on DT135-154; Cairo & Suez low 2
HB	HIS470.10	Egypt-Population, Demography	1E	1E	1E	
DT108-132	HIS471	Sudan	2F	2F	2F	
	HIS472	Sudan-Egyptian Sudan	2E	2E	2F	
	HIS473	Sudan - Anglo-Egyptian Sudan	3E	3E	3E	Low 3
	HIS474	Sudan - Local History and Description	1E	1E	1E	
HB	HIS474.10	Sudan - Population, Demography	0	0	0	
DT160-169	HIS475	North Africa	1F	1F	2F	
DT167-169	HIS476	North Africa - Carthaginian	2E	2E	2E	

Although the goal was to make each summary no longer than two pages, the maximum limit was three, barely long enough to convey an accurate picture of Music or English and American Literature. It was our thinking that any greater length would have defeated the purposes of the summary, but occasionally selectors were hesitant to engage in the editing required for the three page maximum. Several subjects, notably Art History and Economics, required considerable trimming to fit on three pages.

The cost summary, or "price tag" as it became known in Collection Management, was arrived at through a variety of methods. If RLG or NCIP had developed Supplemental Guidelines for the subject, these had been used in the collection assessment. Where the guideline included benchmarks for the various collection levels, an estimate was made of the cost of acquiring the titles needed to reach a certain threshold. Supplemental guidelines were unavailable for many subjects, however. Where this was the case we identified other sources that could be used. Like the guidelines from NCIP or RLG they were fashioned from subject, annual, and serials bibliographies. For a collection to be at a certain level it would need to have a certain percentage of the titles in a given bibliography. This method worked especially well for the sciences. Given the dominance of journal literature, it was possible to identify serials bibliographies to serve as measures for both collection evaluation and budgetary estimates.

Such was not the case for the humanities. For the humanities as well as most of the social sciences, the use of a bibliography (or even a group of bibliographies) for evaluation and budgetary estimates represented little more than taking samples from the collection (or samples from the existing literature on a subject). Furthermore, it was not possible (nor was it desirable) to identify and check a bibliography for every Conspectus subject group. Thus, we turned to the National Shelf-List Count. Through comparing our current holdings and our collection levels with those of other libraries we were able to shore up our evaluation of the collection. Thus use of the Shelf-List Count and the Conspectus in tandem not only bolstered our confidence in the completed collection evaluation but it allowed us to construct meaningful and reasonably accurate budgetary estimates for the cost of developing the Emory collections.

Our methodology was as follows. First, we constructed an estimate for the size of our desired collection. This estimate represented the mean of four to five collections that stood at levels that we would like to attain (see Figure 3 for an example of such a mean). Initially, we had sought to compare ourselves to a peer group of eleven universities identified by our university administration. Since only three of this group participated in the Shelf-List Count, and of those only two (Brown and Johns Hopkins) had embarked upon the Conspectus, we had to expand our list. Any expansion took into consideration only those collections represented in both the RLG Conspectus On-Line and the National Shelf-List Count.

The second element of our formula was the calculation of the cost per title. A number of sources were used in arriving at estimates for material costs. For current materials (books, serials, continuations) we relied upon approval plan reports, serials vendor reports, the *Bowker Annual*, and averages gleaned from our own acquisitions. For retrospective materials, we used the average cost of past purchases, rough averages from selected antiquarian catalogs, and, on one occasion, an estimate from an antiquarian dealer.

The result of multiplying cost per title times the differential between our existing and our desired collecting levels provided us with the "price tag." For each subject, this increased cost was broken down into three areas: new serials, current materials, and retrospective materials. Figures for a particular subject were compared with the allocation for that subject at several of our peer institutions. Many estimates were also checked against national and trade bibliographies. For example, in the case of French History, where we sought to acquire approximately two-thirds of the titles listed in the "Recent Books" section from *French Historical Studies*, we reviewed our estimate to make certain that it would support such a level of acquisition. After review, and subsequent modifications, our estimates were committed to the charts. These charts were, in turn, presented to university administrators. Given the summary nature of the charts, it should be noted that the initial presentation of

FIGURE 3. United States History—National Shelflist Count Comparisons with Other ARL Institutions

SUBJECT	EMORY	BROWN	J.HOPKINS	U of MI	U of GA	U VA	Berk	LC
E1-139 America-General, Indians, Discovery and Exploration	3225	3651	3733	7340	5833	3628	9159	24056
E140-200 U.S.-General History, Elements in the Population, Colonial History	7025	7119	6461	12644	8063	9904	10295	33576
E201-299 American Revolution	1200	1494	1333	2152	1531	1901	1266	9850
E301-440 Post-Revolution to Civil War	2275	2799	1589	3103	2290	4087	2363	12513
E441-655 Slavery, Civil War	4125	9080	3563	4785	4485	4163	3554	21428
E656-876 Late 19th Century, 20th Century	4250	3759	3051	6825	4464	4515	4675	15133
F1-105 U.S. Local History, N. England, Atlantic States	2725	14173	2929	3886	3140	4515	4717	35551
F206-475 The South, Gulf States, Old South	5665	2307	2342	3920	8769	8200	3436	25312

Class								
F476-705 Old Northwest, The West	1950	1761	1128	3860	2135	2837	3487	20105
F721-854 Rocky Mountains, New Southwest, Pacific Northwest	775	724	412	1316	1150	932	1493	6892
F856-975 Pacific States and U.S. Possessions	800	948	473	1741	1230	1099	3228	10167
TOTAL	34015	47815	27014	51572	43090	45781	47673	214583

TOTALS SUMMARY

EMORY COLLECTION	34015
MEAN COLLECTION (excluding LC)	43410
DIFFERENTIAL	9395

the charts involved a thorough explanation of the methodology used in our collection assessment and in the preparation of budget estimates.

CONCLUSIONS

The creation of charts, summarizing Conspectus results and expectations for collection development, made the Conspectus comprehensible and thereby, useful for the library and the university. Within the library, the process of developing cost estimates for the summary charts gave selectors a start on knowing what and how much to select, instead of having only an intuitive understanding of the CCI. The summaries also served as a quick introduction to the state of the collection for new library administrators. A new Director of Libraries and a new Director of Collection Management were able to use Conspectus summaries as a point of reference in establishing communication about the collection, both within the library and externally.

On the university level, the results of the Conspectus evaluation as presented in executive summary form have been tangible. Using the findings of the collection evaluation to back up budget requests, the library has received increases for current and retrospective materials. The Conspectus has been referred to by departments doing self studies and as part of reports to accreditation teams.

Finally, it has provided a basis of dialogue with university administration in the consideration of the library requirements of establishing new academic programs, appointing new faculty, and the like.

REFERENCES

1. Nancy E. Gwinn and Paul H. Mosher, "Coordinating Collection Development: The RLG Conspectus," *College & Research Libraries* 44:128-40 (Mar. 1983).

2. Jutta Reed-Scott, *Manual for the North American Inventory of Research Library Collections*, Rev. ed., September 1988.

3. Peggy Forcier, "Building Collections Together: The Pacific Northwest Conspectus," *Library Journal*, 113:43-45 (Apr. 15, 1988).

4. Anthony W. Ferguson, Joan Grant, and Joel S. Rutstein, "The RLG Conspectus: Its Uses and Benefits, *College & Research Libraries* 49:197-206 (May 1988).

5. David Henige, "Epistemological Dead End and Ergonomic Disaster? The North American Collections Inventory Project," *The Journal of Academic Librarianship*, 13:209-213 (September 1987).

6. Ross Atkinson, "The Language of the Levels: Reflections on the Communication of Collection Development Policy," *College & Research Libraries* 46:140-149 (March 1986).

7. *Ibid.*, p. 141.

8. American Library Association. Collection Development Committee. *Guidelines for Collection Development*, 1979. pp. 3-5.

9. *Ibid.*

10. *Ibid.*, p. 143.

11. A complete account of the collection assessment project has been written by Kathy Tezla, Social Science Coordinator, and will not be repeated here.

EVALUATING THE ACQUISITIONS FUNCTION

Variations on a Theme: Evaluating the Acquisitions Department

Carol Fleishauer
Marilyn G. McSweeney

SUMMARY. Different criteria for judging the quality of an acquisitions department are likely to exist in various library units — collection development, public services, and library administration. The article describes these criteria and suggests ways to fulfill them. The authors maintain that an acquisitions department must ultimately be judged by its ability to effectively balance its responses to the multiple, and often conflicting, criteria imposed by the various units with which it interacts.

Do you know how good your acquisitions department is? If you are a bibliographer, a reference librarian, a cataloger, or a library budget officer, probably not. You may well be like the proverbial blind man describing the elephant. Even as a technical services ad-

Carol Fleishauer is Associate Director for Collection Management and Technical Services and Marilyn G. McSweeney is Head, Acquisitions Department at Massachusetts Institute of Technology Libraries, 14S-312, Cambridge, MA 02139.

61

ministrator, you may have a partial and skewed view of the quality
of service provided. Each of the groups represented by these various positions will judge the effectiveness of the acquisitions department by different, and often conflicting, criteria. Where does the
acquisitions department fit in the fulfillment of the mission of each
unit, as well as in support of the overall mission of the library?
What are the criteria used by each of these units to evaluate acquisitions service? The total effectiveness of the department will be measured by how well it meets all of these criteria, and whether it can
achieve the appropriate balance when there are conflicts. Since obtaining material quickly, efficiently, and at minimal cost has always
been a critical component in satisfying the library's primary mission, a continuing, well-informed evaluation of this service department is an essential administrative activity. That assessment should
be based on a thorough understanding of the demands on the acquisitions unit from the various library units, as well as on more general and formal evaluation techniques.

The most fundamental organizational relationship for an acquisitions department is the relationship to the collection development
effort, wherever that takes place within the organization. Gail Kennedy has referred to collection development as the "head or brain of
the collection body" and acquisitions as "its hands and feet."[1] Joe
Hewitt referred to the position of acquisitions in the library organization as "a vale of humility between two mountains of conceit":
collection development and cataloging! He described the acquisitions department, thus, as being at the core of a research library's
mission, contributing to systematic development of collections and
high quality bibliographic control.[2]

Whether the desired materials can be acquired and whether they
are acquired at the lowest possible cost are the primary criteria by
which collection development staff will assess the effectiveness of
the acquisitions department. In this case, there is tension between
the two criteria imposed by a single library unit. Attempting to acquire materials at the lowest cost may jeopardize the ability to acquire them at all. For an acquisitions department to best satisfy the
needs of collection development in a given library, it will be important to arrive at a mutual understanding of the relative values of
these two criteria. In an environment of short print runs, speed of

acquisition is also becoming an important collection development concern because it is becoming a means of *assuring* acquisition. In the case of science and technology monographs, for instance, where acquisition of out-of-print materials is extremely problematic, if a library doesn't acquire quickly, it may not be able to acquire at all.

While these are the general criteria for judging the department, the activities which lead to successful fulfillment of them are multiple, complex, and overlapping. Is pre-order searching precise enough to avoid unintentional duplication? Are orders prepared accurately enough to ensure fulfillment? Are appropriate decisions made regarding ordering directly or ordering through a vendor? Are vendor choice and continuing vendor evaluation effective? Do the staff in the department understand vendor reports well enough to respond correctly? Are claims submitted regularly? Are approval plans managed effectively? Are procedures designed to interface properly with accounting to provide adequate and timely budget information?

In the overall assessment of acquisitions performance, collection development staff may value service as much as assured acquisition of material and good price. Assessing service, is subjective and imprecise. As in any service operation, however, the more the service can be individualized the more highly it will be valued. The ultimate individualized acquisitions service has been provided in large research libraries where the acquisitions staff (or perhaps only the order staff) are organizationally a part of individual curators' offices, rather than a part of a central acquisitions department. There is likely to be some loss of efficiency in this structure, however, and it is not supportable except in the largest libraries. A compromise that still provides a strong service emphasis is to divide staff assignments in a central acquisitions department according to the subject assignments of the individual bibliographers, so that each bibliographer gives his or her orders to a specified staff member with whom a close working relationship is established. This is likely to provide both actual and perceived improved service over the model in which all orders come into a central point in the acquisitions department and are divided among staff randomly.

Another important factor in achieving a high service rating from collection development staff is responsiveness to special requests,

such as the use of a specified vendor for a given order, the establishment of a procedure for review of received materials by those bibliographers who want hands-on experience of the collection they are
building, or a telephone campaign to discover the availability of
materials with elusive bibliographic verification. Such special services inevitably are labor intensive. Sound judgement must be used
by the department head in balancing these special service requests
with the ability to maintain effectiveness in the more regular department activities.

While speed of acquisition is now becoming important as a collection development criterion, it has always been the most important criterion in a public services assessment of the acquisitions department. Hewitt described the many constraints on timely delivery
of materials: poor dealer performance, short print runs, inaccurate
dealer reports, inaccurate pre-publication announcements, pre-pay-
ment requirements, postal strikes, and accounting and auditing requirements.[3] To minimize these impediments the acquisitions department head and the staff must have a sound understanding of
publisher and vendor business practices, efficient in-house procedures, and good relationships with library and university accounting
offices. The most obvious needs for timeliness, when the acquisitions department will be harshly judged if it does not perform well,
are cases of rush and reserve materials. There is no more blatant
instance of an academic library's failure to meet the needs of its
public than the failure to have reserve materials ready for course
work. Although success in this area depends equally on faculty and
public service staff, who typically coordinate the requests, the acquisitions department must develop reliable sources and procedures
for obtaining these special materials. Developing a good relationship with the buyer in the university bookstore can contribute to
success in this area, as can the use of a specific vendor who may be
able to provide expeditious service for these materials. From a different perspective, the university bookstore often provides a common source of public discontent with library acquisitions. When
users see a new title displayed in the bookstore, it is difficult for
them to understand why the library does not yet have a copy. The

most rational description of the national book distribution system is unlikely to persuade these disgruntled library users.

The public services staff will continue to evaluate the acquisitions department primarily by timeliness — whether it has acquired the materials by the time users demand them. In the modern age of automated acquisitions systems, however, additional evaluative criteria are emerging. Are the records describing on order and in-process materials integrated into the on-line public catalog? Are the records adequate, correct, and consistent with the rest of the catalog file? Are there adequate procedures to retrieve in-process items and provide them to users in a timely fashion? These new criteria may produce an extra demand on the acquisitions staff and they require careful planning and balancing if the traditional services are not to suffer. The ultimate interaction between user and acquisitions staff occurs when a persistent user bypasses the reference desk retrieval mechanisms and strides into the acquisitions department demanding an in-process item. While this has happened occasionally in the past, occurrences have increased with the availability of acquisitions records in the on-line catalog, so acquisitions staff may now need to develop some of the finesse and skill that public services staff have long used in dealing directly with the user community.

While collection development and public services can be thought of as the two major "clients" or "customers" of the acquisitions department's services, there are two other library units that must cooperate or at least coordinate with acquisitions to fulfill their own service functions. These are the catalog department and the accounting office. Each has its basis for judging the effectiveness of the acquisitions department.

In the flow of in-process materials, acquisitions and catalog departments perform as partners in service. The catalog department has historically relied on pre-order searching information and cataloging instructions carried on the order slip. With automation, the dependence has grown. It is now not uncommon for searching for copy to take place in the acquisitions department, and, typically, the record established at the time of ordering serves as a provisional record (sometimes for months or years) until the item is cataloged. Some fixed and variable fields will be carried from the provisional record into the permanent record. In this environment, the catalog department is likely to judge the acquisitions department by the quality of its searching and record creation. Incomplete or inaccurate searching notations will result in the conclusion on the part of catalog department staff that they must perform redundant searching. Inaccurate or inadequate on-line order records may result in a climate wherein catalog department staff will be highly sensitive to and critical of errors created in a department using entry level staff or students who receive less exacting training in the cataloging rules. Sound planning and communication are necessary to establish procedures which are cost-effective for the entire technical services work flow and which make appropriate use of the distinctive expertise of the two departments. Catalog department staff are also likely to evaluate the acquisitions department by the quality of its various files, although they may be using the files for very different purposes from those for which they were intended. Another criterion may be the quantity and evenness of work flow, even though there may be a rational acknowledgement that the acquisitions department often has little control over this. Given the usual physical proximity of catalog and acquisitions departments, these will be powerful judgements in spite of the fact that this is not a client-server relationship.

The accounting office with which the acquisitions department interacts, whether in the library, the parent institution, or both, will likewise have its own standards for evaluating acquisitions work. To be favorably judged by accounting staff, notations on invoices forwarded for payment will have to be clear, consistent, correct, and forwarded in a timely manner. Knowledge of the practices of the accounting office should be sufficient to reduce questions to an acceptable level. Exploring vendor or publisher options for consolidated billing, taking advantage of deposit accounts when appropriate, or making certain that invoicing profiles meet the standardized needs of the accounting staff will contribute much to a smoother relationship. More critically, order, receipt, and payment records must satisfy institutional auditing requirements. Encumbrance and expenditure records and practices must be sufficient to ensure expenditure of all funds by the end of the fiscal year in many libraries, while contingency plans may also be necessary for spending one-time, year-end funding.

The technical services administrator's view of the acquisitions department should be a "sighted" one in contrast to the various blind man's views of single library units. This view must be comprehensive, almost omniscient, extending across organizational boundaries and outside the libraries. The administrator needs to be aware of the number and diversity of relationships that acquisitions has with other library units and staff—many of whom are relatively uninformed about the nature and scope of acquisitions work as it relates to any department outside their own. Weighing the demands made by the various library units on the department and the success with which the department meets those demands will form a critical part of the administrator's assessment. This should be based on the ability of the department to balance its responses to the various demands appropriately, and cannot rest solely on the experience of any one powerful library unit. The administrator's comprehensive view must also acknowledge the acquisitions department's internal goals relating to productivity, efficiency, and the streamlined flow of orders, materials, and invoices. The desire to establish goals in a service department, such as acquisitions, must necessarily be balanced not only with the needs of the library units served but also with the requirements of the external publishers and vendors who receive the acquisitions orders and supply the materials and invoices. Their practices and priorities must be understood and factored into the goal-setting process and the assessment. The role of the acquisitions department as facilitator between the library units and the publisher/vendor community is one that requires a high degree of flexibility, expediency, and adaptability in meeting conditions set by a variety of other agencies, both internal and external to the library.[4] Not only must this situation be understood by the library administration, but success in fostering a shared understanding of the publishing business among the library units should also be a factor in evaluating the department.

The library administration will have additional criteria. Some of its expectations will be those it has of any department: sound departmental planning and reporting, effective personnel management, appropriate utilization of automation. A criterion that is less common for other units relates to acquisitions' role as institutional representative with outside agencies. It is appropriate to evaluate the department on how well it fulfills the ethical behavior standards established by the institution and the library profession.

There may also be "text-book" attempts to assess the department. In *The Measurement and Evaluation of Library Services*, F.W. Lancaster devoted a chapter to technical services. He stated that while theoretically technical services departments could be evaluated from two viewpoints, their internal efficiency and their long-range effect on public services, little has actually been done to evaluate the latter.[5] He described numerous approaches to measuring efficiency: calculation of the staff time involved in various processing steps, the time elapsed from point of order or receipt to shelving, and the productivity of staff in various processes. Comparisons can be made of the results of such measurements within one institution over time or between similar institutions. An example of the former which was carried out at Iowa State University was reported at the January, 1989, meeting of RTSD Technical Services Administrators of Medium-Sized Research Libraries Discussion Group, by Dilys Morris. Technical services staff time used for receiving/checking-in, claiming, searching orders, copy cataloging, recataloging, authority work, binding preparation, marking/labeling, revision, card filing, OCLC edit/input, and revision, was sampled regularly from April, 1987, through September, 1988, with an intent to continue sampling indefinitely.[6] Variations over time in number of hours within each category and in percentage of total staff time used for each category will provide useful management information. An example of a comparison of similar institutions was reported to the RTSD Technical Services Directors of Large Research Libraries Discussion Group, by Cynthia Gozzi of Stanford University Libraries, in 1987. Gross calculations of number of items processed per number of staff were calculated for twenty-three institutions in the categories of monographic acquisitions, monographic cataloging, serials acquisitions, serials cataloging, shelf preparation work, binding preparation, and binding.[7] This kind of comparison can demonstrate whether productivity in a technical services department varies substantially from that of similar departments in colleague institutions. It requires careful follow-up to determine whether there are legitimate environmental factors contributing to the results. Differences in automated systems and in number of hours worked per week provide only the most obvious variations which will affect differences in productivity.

While public service units undoubtedly face more stressful situations in dealing directly with the demands of a broad population of library users, the acquisitions department is unique in the number of library units that depend directly on its services. Magrill and Hickey recognized this in their emphasis on "systems evaluation" of acquisitions processes.[8] There are definite tensions which result from the various expectations of the different groups. The insistence of a bibliographer that a specialized vendor be used for certain materials may conflict with the accounting office's desire to process as few invoices as possible. Public services staff's opinion that popular items should be purchased in the university bookstore as soon as they are available there may compromise the bibliographer's desire to obtain materials at the lowest possible cost. The technical services administrator's emphasis on high productivity can jeopardize a close service relationship between acquisitions staff and bibliographers. Catalog department standards for searching and record creation carried out in the acquisitions department may result in the inability to meet the productivity expectations of administration.

Hewitt states that ". . . it is entirely proper in the typical research library organization that the role of acquisitions be to serve, to accommodate, and to adjust."[9] The final evaluation of an acquisitions department must rest on how well its many accommodations and adjustments support the unique mission and goals of the library as a whole, as well as the objectives of the many individual units with which it interacts.

REFERENCES

1. Gail A. Kennedy, "The Relationship between Acquisitions and Collection Development," *Library Acquisitions: Practice and Theory* 7, no.3:226 (1983).

2. Joe A. Hewitt, "On the Nature of Acquisitions," *Library Resources & Technical Services* 3,no.2:10-11 (April, 1989).

3. Ibid., p.113.

4. Ibid., p.111.

5. F.W. Lancaster, *The Measurement and Evaluation of Library Services* (Arlington, VA: Information Resources Press, 1977), pp. 264, 269.

6. Dilys Morris, "Time and Cost Studies in Technical Services." RTSD Technical Services Administration of Medium-Sized Research Libraries, A.L.A. Convention, Washington, 7 Jan, 1989.

7. Cynthia I. Gozzi, "Stanford Survey of Technical Services Staffing Levels." RTSD Technical Services Directors of Large Research Libraries, A.L.A. Convention, San Francisco, 26 June, 1987.

8. Rose Mary Magrill and Doralyn J. Hickey, *Acquisitions Management and Collection Development* (Chicago: American Library Association, 1984), p. 210.

9. Hewitt, p. 111.

Evaluating Acquisitions Service: New Concepts and Changing Perceptions

Carol E. Chamberlain

SUMMARY. The general concept of evaluation of the acquisitions function is based on a traditional view of acquisitions as a support for the building of library collections, and as a transaction-based operation full of routine tasks and detailed procedures. This concept has led to conflicts in the ways the quality and effectiveness of the process are judged. As the focus of libraries has shifted from collection building to providing access to information, the focus of acquisitions has shifted as well. Acquisitions is viewed as a service to meet the information needs of library users, and new developments mark this changed perception. There is strong emphasis on the management function, on a collaboration of effort among libraries, and on access to information as well as ownership of resources. Acquisitions service is evaluated in new ways in light of its multiple missions.

Like other library technical services, acquisitions has a traditional function which is central to the library organization but largely undiscernible to the user. The range of functions generally includes the procurement of all formats of materials and other resources including print, microform, software, etc. The concept of evaluating acquisitions varies with a given perspective, particularly whether one is looking from within the operation or from outside the operation. These perspectives lead to conflicts between different frames of reference and different expectations. This traditional concept of evaluation, however valid in today's library environment, is now incomplete. Several factors in the acquisitions environment

Carol E. Chamberlain is Head, Acquisitions Department, Pennsylvania State University Libraries, E506 Pattee, University Park, PA 16802.

have changed the focus of evaluation in recent years. These factors are: (1) the changes in business practices and in the publishing industry which have brought about a greater focus on the management function; (2) a strengthening of the acquisitions profession toward more collaboration among libraries and agencies; and (3) the trend toward access to library resources versus ownership of library resources. These developments are changing the perception of acquisition service and how to evaluate it. In contrast to the dire warnings that acquisitions departments will disappear in the age of electronic resources, it is more likely that they will be here in the future, and that they are beginning to contribute from a position of strength rather than a position of weakness. These changes may indeed bring about a greater understanding of the value of the acquisitions process and an end to the conflicts.

PERSPECTIVES ON EVALUATION

The acquisitions function consists of multiple transactions of verifying requests, placing orders, monitoring funds, processing receipts and invoices, and creating and maintaining appropriate records to track each transaction. Because it is process oriented, an internal evaluation of how well the acquisitions function is performed is typically viewed from the aggregate, e.g., the number of orders placed within a given period of time, the number of receipts, the number of claims, etc. It may be formal, i.e., a standard which is established and measured, or informal through observation (the staff is able to "keep up" with the order requests). In the past "the emphasis has tended to be more upon accuracy than speed" but with the increasing complexity of publishing, including shorter print runs for many books, and with automation and budget crises resulting in staffing cuts in many libraries, speed is also a critical factor.[1]

Evaluation of acquisitions by individuals outside the department such as selectors or library users is often informal and is typically based on a single transaction rather than the aggregate whole. All acquisitions departments deal with irate users who are critical of the entire operation simply because one item on order has not yet arrived. While acquisitions staff can often minimize these occurrences and shift priorities accordingly by predicting which titles will be in high demand or which selector expects faster turnaround, it is not always possible to anticipate all circumstances. Much of this is based on the nature of book and journal publishing (over which the acquisitions department has little or no control), and on the nature of the acquisitions operation.

Operational Focus

The nature of the acquisitions operation is typically given to streamlining procedures and tasks. The emphasis within a unit, whether the tasks are preorder searching, order placement, recording receipt, creating item records, returning duplicates, etc., is on consistency of workflow in order to achieve the best combination of accuracy and speed. A typical workflow includes the principle of "first in first out." As Kantor states, ". . . some aspects of placing purchase orders can be done on almost a pure FIFO basis. The receiving of books can generally be done on a pure FIFO basis."[2] The key works are "almost" and "generally," as all acquisitions staff know there are constant expectations which result in abrupt shifts in priority, such as special offers with immediate deadlines and personal requests for follow up on special titles. A unit's daily activities can easily be judged by the number of transactions completed and while accommodating expectations is critical to effective service, they are apt to skew production standards. The number of requests for exceptions to the FIFO workflow has a negative impact on the numbers of orders or receipts that can be processed during the same timeframe. The more time spent in responding to exceptional needs, the longer it takes to complete the regular ongoing tasks. In evaluating responsive service, individuals outside the acquisitions department tend to evaluate highly the granting of exceptions to the established operations. These exceptions typically relate to an individual transaction and may require several hours of investigation. Having fewer staff to do more complex tasks, acquisitions librarians tend to minimize the special services performed in acquisitions because the overall effect is detrimental to the ongoing work.

Measuring Effectiveness

Evaluating the cost effectiveness of acquisitions service typically involves a number of factors such as the costs associated with automation, supplier selection, preorder bibliographic verification, supplier performance, discounts and service charges, one-time versus standing orders, approval plans, etc. Acquisition departments tend to focus on the method of procurement and the simplification of tasks such as verification. Local studies have been undertaken to establish the average cost of acquiring an item.[3] Since most libraries acquire through vendors and agents, evaluating the performance of suppliers is a primary element. Guidelines for the evaluation of vendors have been established.[4] Acquisitions professionals tend to see all the variables as important parts of the whole. Pricing (including discounts and service charges) is factored into achieving effectiveness but it is rarely the highest priority. However, the value placed on acquisition service is sometimes exclusively related to "the price paid" for books, journals or other resources. Purchasing agents who govern the expenditure of funds for an institution may not be knowledgeable about library acquisitions and effective means of procurement. This lack of understanding may lead to the questioning of monies paid to vendors for "extras" such as service charges. Of course, acquisitions librarians want to pay the lowest charge possible, but the bottom line cannot always be just the dollar amounts on the invoice. Fulfillment is critical and the typical library user does not care whether the price is low if the item is not acquired and made accessible when it is needed.

The institutional perspective on cost effectiveness extends to the process of bids. As acquisitions librarians well know, the lowest bid may win the deal, but not necessarily signify a quality acquisitions process. The local institutional requirements have a major impact on how cost effective an acquisitions operation can be achieved.[5] Each organization follows its own financial regulations as well as the general accounting principles. For example, prepayments to vendors through deposit accounts or early payment plans, which are considered effective means to get credits or discounts in order to decrease or contain the costs of acquisitions, may not be permitted by some organizations given their investment strategies. In such a case, the investment benefit to the institution as a whole (from investing the money itself for the period of time rather than paying it to a vendor to invest) takes precedence over the cost containment strategies of the library. It is hoped that most organizations see the benefits of passing along such rewards to the library, although it is doubtful that this is a common practice.

Auditing requirements and the controls imposed by adherence to a fiscal year budget cycle are other examples of the institutional perspective. The annual "use it or lose it" syndrome requires some acquisitions departments to expend considerable time and effort to ensure the expenditure of the budget at the close of the fiscal year or risk losing money. An even greater risk lies in the implication of not expending the budget which could signal to uninformed institutional leaders that the library does not need all the money allocated for acquisitions. Effectiveness is often compromised by using devices such as overencumbering funds by a certain percentage in order to cover those orders which will not be received prior to the end of the fiscal year. This adds another dimension to evaluation, as the levels of overencumbered funds must be monitored closely so that the carryover encumbrances from the previous fiscal year budget will not eat up the next year's funds.

The different ways that acquisitions tends to be evaluated internally, by those in the department and externally, by individuals outside the department, can lead to conflicts. As Hewitt has noted, acquisitions is often seen as a superficially routine and simple process, but by nature accommodating and flexible to meet demands largely out of its control. He also has noted, however, that there is actually an underlying complexity.[6] These views can be extended to evaluation as well. What is judged as a good or effective acquisitions operation tends to be based on the traditional focus of acquisitions. Much of that tradition is still valid, but it is incomplete in light of several new developments affecting the profession.

THE TRADITIONAL MISSION

The traditional view holds that acquisitions supports the collection building in libraries particularly during the time when the focus was on building larger collections. The mission of acquisitions then was ". . . to insure that materials selected for addition to the library's collection are received as efficiently, inexpensively and quickly as possible."[7] Labor-intensive methods were lauded in an attempt to achieve a perfect process of procurement without claims and vendor status reports.[8] With the economic crises that have resulted in budget cuts and with the advent of automated systems and electronic publishing, this view is no longer true. It is widely acknowledged that the era of large collection building is over, and acquisitions is no longer seen as simply a support function for building collections, but is an active participant in information management.

Despite the radical changes, acquisitions has continued to be a poorly understood process and its contributions have been largely neglected in the literature.[9] As noted in 1989, acquisitions librarianship has "been bound by a narrowly defined view of traditional librarianship, a service profession in which 'business' has sometimes been treated as a dirty word."[10] In many libraries, the acquisitions department has a central role in activities such as the budget allocation process, but it has been largely up to the acquisitions professionals to educate others about what they do beyond the simplified order and receipt routines.[11]

How does this reflect on the role of evaluation? Because the focus in the past has been on acquisitions as a routine support activity, little attention has been paid to the formal evaluation of most aspects of acquisitions other than vendor performance. Evaluation has largely been directed at the selection of materials and assessment of collections.[12] Published library policies traditionally have been guides for collection evaluation.[13]

EVALUATION: CHANGE FOR THE BETTER

In 1977 Schenck lamented that "librarians have exhibited a tendency to remain aloof from the business world."[14] There is a relative isolation of the profession from other library operations as well as from the business world. However, the characteristics of acquisitions evaluation to focus on the practical operations and real costs have prepared the profession well to deal with the major changes which have had an impact on all areas of the library.[15] The changes include severe economic crises, library automation, and electronic resources. These changes have added a new dimension to the concept of evaluation. It is expending the role of acquisitions to focus on (1) the management function, (2) on collaboration as opposed to isolation, and (3) on access as well as acquisitions.

Management Focus

The changes in the publishing industry have led acquisitions departments to focus more on managing the "business of acquisitions" than dealing with the details of operations. The IRS Thor Power Tool tax ruling forced publishers toward shorter print runs and smaller print runs and smaller inventories of backlist titles. The inflation rate of library materials prices has risen higher than the general inflation rate. Also, the unfair policies of publishers in terms of differential pricing of journals to different library markets are well documented, as are the extreme price increases of a relatively few major professional and scientific journal publishers. Additionally, the library community has witnessed the introduction of microcomputer software and machine-readable data files to the range of resources provided. All of these changes have resulted in a re-evaluation of acquisitions policies to respond to new developments. For example, in order to obtain books before they are out-of-print, there is a renewed emphasis on approval plans, prepublication ordering and OP services.[16] Acquisitions librarians are actively evaluating the prices paid for books and journals and are taking a leadership role in exposing the exploitation by a handful of publishers, often by means of published studies and national organizations.[17] They are evaluating legal implications and the terms of license agreements, and negotiating contracts with software producers on a regular basis. In fact, the concept of purchasing resources has been radically changed as acquisitions departments are forced to deal with purchase requirements which no longer result in ownership. The range of services provided has increased so much that acquisitions is ". . . in many ways closer in function to outside purchasing departments, contracts management offices, accounts payable and receivable operations. . . ."[18]

Acquisitions librarians also have taken on the role of consumer advocate as they measure the costs of restrictive publisher policies such as requiring direct purchases. As competition for library acquisitions dollars increase, the acquisitions librarian not only continues to evaluate a book vendor's or subscription agent's performance, but also demands up-front deals such as guaranteed discounts and extra services such as management reports and price projections.

With the maturation of automated acquisition systems, the focus of automation is more on the management function and less on the operational process. The need for sophisticated system support for management information such as fund accounting controls, analyses by country of acquisition, by subject area, and by order type has been documented.[19] The importance of management information to the evaluation of acquisition service has grown tremendously in the past several years as budget cuts and changes in the publishing industry have renewed emphasis on finding ways to extend purchasing power. Much information can be gleaned from an acquisitions system, including the analysis of costs and forecasting of price increases.[20] As the focus on collection building has lessened, the focus on effective analysis has deepened. Acquisitions librarians are "active participants in the marketplace."[21] This active presence has led to less isolation and more collaboration as a professional group. This is the second way that acquisitions has changed.

Collaboration

With a vocal participation and growing influence in areas such as publishing and library-related technology, acquisitions librarians are beginning to work together. As noted earlier, isolation has been a predominant characteristic not only because of the traditional perception of acquisitions as primarily a non-professional activity, but also because of the highly individualistic institutional purchasing requirements.[22] Magrill notes that in terms of the overall operation of the library "the acquisitions unit can operate in isolation less than any other. . . ."[23]

Even with the advent of automation, the perception has persisted that each acquisitions operation in each library is unique. Acquisitions has suffered in the past from a lack of standards, such as those developed for cataloging. Cataloging has been transformed through the adoption of the MARC standard. The development of the BISAC and SISAC standards as well as other industry standards pertaining to transmission of publication data has led to greater awareness of the similarities of non-bibliographic acquisitions data and the possibility of more cooperative standards.[24] Still, the lack of a corresponding MARC-like standard for data elements in an acquisitions record in the automated system has made it more difficult for librarians to develop shared principles of evaluation. User groups established for the purpose of sharing information and providing feedback to the various commercial automated systems vendors have assumed an effective role.

There is a growing variety of formal organizations and informal groups that serve to give a greater voice. In addition to system user groups, special interest groups and advisory boards representing acquisitions librarians from all types of libraries have been formed by publishers and vendors. This recognition of acquisitions as a market influence was virtually unheard of just a few years ago, and it had been prompted by a growing number of acquisitions librarians who have joined the ranks as active consultants in the processes associated with publishing and distribution.

Access and Ownership

Evaluation of the acquisitions function is changing in a third way, to include a focus on access to information in addition to ownership. The issues can be characterized as access to electronic information, document delivery and resource sharing. Before the large-scale development of electronic resources such as full-text databases, resource sharing was and continues to be a practical alternative for some libraries. But as Dunlap asked in 1977, "How can we be sure that the money spent on sharing programs would not be better spent on materials to be housed locally?"[25] That same question is relevant today as user-prompted on-demand acquisitions is becoming more prevalent in libraries and as document delivery services are established.

The impact on acquisitions of document delivery services is great. Documents (such as technical reports or journal article reprints) may be purchased directly for a single user rather than purchased for the library collection. Items in the collection theoretically are available to all library users whereas the single documents are "owned" by the individual user. Additionally, there may be no intervention or review of the request by collection development specialists. This may not be much different than the more traditional interlibrary loan activity, except that the costs are greater, the purchases typically are made from the acquisitions budget, and the items are not obtained from other libraries at consortium rates, but from commercial sources. Evaluation of such an acquisition service presents a challenge since the choices of supply are limited and in some cases the acquisitions department may be completely bypassed, at least at the ordering stage. This development leaves more questions than answers at this time. How are the costs for such a service measured against user need? How does acquisitions define effective budget management and determine the appropriate distribution of funds? How can a balance be achieved between user needs on demand and long-term support for collection development goals?

On-line access to electronic information resources is another challenge to acquisitions. As libraries expand their mission to users to include the provision of full-text databases and electronic journals for direct access, will acquisitions be out of the service loop entirely? Given its expertise with the business aspects of the information industry, its experience with transaction-based operations and the budget management activities, it is likely that the acquisitions department will continue to have a role in managing the library's transition from ownership of resources to access to resources.

CONCLUSION

Acquisitions is still in the business of "shaping collections," but there are new ways of judging the quality of acquisitions service.[26] The traditional functions are important but they have been joined by new issues which have inspired change. The management responsibility is critical to acquisition service as the international publishing market and the information industry grow more complex. Collaboration on several different fronts will bring enhanced productivity, practical application of standards and strong influence to bear on related markets. As information access plays a larger role, there will be a greater concentration on contract negotiation and cost assessment. It is hoped that these developments will bring about an improved understanding and fewer conflicts among library colleagues. The challenge to acquisitions will be to "rechannel acquisitions expertise" to better serve its multiple missions.[27]

REFERENCES

1. Rose Mary Magrill and Doralyn J. Hickey, *Acquisitions Management and Collection Development in Libraries.* (Chicago: American Library Association, 1984): 207.

2. Paul B. Kantor, *Objective Performance Measures for Academic and Research Libraries.* (Washington, DC: Association of Research Libraries, 1984): 67.

3. Gary M. Pitkin, *Cost-Effective Technical Services.* (New York: Neal-Schuman Publishers, Inc., 1989).

4. *Guide to Performance Evaluation of Library Materials Vendors.* (Chicago: American Library Association, 1988).

5. Barbara J. Henn, "Acquisitions Management: The Infringing Roles of Acquisitions Librarians and Subject Specialists—An Historical Perspective," in *Advances in Library Administration and Organization* (Greenwich, CT: JAI Press, Inc., vol. 8, 1989): 119.

6. Joe A. Hewitt, "On the Nature of Acquisitions," *Library Resources and Technical Services* 33 no. 2 (April 1989): 107.

7. William Z. Schenck, "Acquiring Library Materials as Efficiently, Inexpensively, and Quickly as Possible: Exploring Possibilities Within 'The Impossible Dream,'" *Library Acquisitions: Practice and Theory* 1 (1977): 194.

8. Franciska Safran, "Defensive Ordering," *Library Acquisitions: Practice and Theory* 3 no. 1 (1979): 5-8.

9. Robert J. Dukes, Jr., "Faculty/Library Relations in Acquisitions and Collection Development: The Faculty Perspective," *Library Acquisitions: Practice and Theory* 7 (1983): 221-224.

10. Peggy Johnson, "The Business of Acquisitions," *Technicalities* 9 no. 6 (June 1989): 5.

11. Pam Cenzer, "Library/Faculty Relations in the Acquisitions and Collection Development Process," *Library Acquisitions: Practice and Theory* 7 (1983): 215-219.

12. Magrill, *Acquisitions Management and Collection Development in Libraries.* p. 205.

13. Elizabeth Futas, *Library Acquisition Policies and Procedures* (Phoenix, AZ: The Oryx Press, 1984): 503.

14. Schenck, "Acquiring Library Materials as Efficiently, Inexpensively, and Quickly as Possible," p. 195.

15. Hewitt, "On the Nature of Acquisitions," p. 118.

16. Mary H. Loe, "Thor Tax Ruling After 5 Years: Its Effect on Publishing and Libraries," *Library Acquisitions: Practice and Theory* 10 (1986): 217.

17. See *Newsletter on Serials Pricing Issues*, published by the American Library Association and available in electronic format.

18. Sherman Hayes, "Let me Count the Ways: Information Acquisition Accounting," *The Bottom Line* 3 no. 3 (1989): 30.

19. Colleen F. Hyslop, "Maintaining Business as Usual With Vendors While Implementing the INNOVACQ Automated Acquisitions System: Potential Conflicts Between System Capabilities and the Needs of Libraries and Vendors," *Library Acquisitions: Practice and Theory* 12 (1988): 105-108.

20. Carol E. Chamberlain, "Fiscal Planning in Academic Libraries: The Role of the Automated Acquisitions System," in *Advances in Library Administration and Organization* (Greenwich, CT: JAI Press, Inc., vol. 6, 1986): 141-152.

21. Johnson, "The Business of Acquisitions," p. 6.

22. Karen A. Schmidt, "The Acquisitions Process in Research Libraries: A Survey of ARL Libraries' Acquisitions Departments," *Library Acquisitions: Practice and Theory* 11 no. 1 (1987): 35-44.

23. Magrill, *Acquisitions Management and Collection Development in Libraries.* p. 210.

24. Joseph W. Barker, "Library-to-Vendor Electronic Order Transmission Today," *Library Acquisitions: Practice and Theory* 13 (1989): 275-279.

25. Connie Dunlap, "Resource Sharing and Cooperative Acquisitions: A Guardedly Optimistic View," *Library Acquisitions: Practice and Theory* 1 (1977): 202.

26. Craig S. Likness, "The Creative Use of Acquisitions Mechanisms in the College Library," *Collection Management* 12 no. 1/2 (1990): 4.

27. Edwin Brownrigg, Clifford Lynch and Mary Engle, "Technical Services in the Age of Electronic Publishing," *Library Resources and Technical Services* 28 no. 1 (January/March 1984): 66.

The Acquisitions/Collection Development Departments as Service Units in Academic Libraries: A Less Traditional Evaluative Criterion

Stephen Bosch
Chris Sugnet

SUMMARY. Traditionally, the acquisition functions of most libraries have been centered in technical services and the acquisitions department has not been viewed as a unit that provides a high level of service to patrons. Although the primary focus of an acquisitions department may not include direct service to the public, service is an important by-product of the activity of an acquisitions department. This paper will focus on the service value of the acquisitions function in an academic library. Since the function of collection development units and acquisitions units frequently overlap, some observations may apply as well to collection development! The academic library may be the primary focus of discussion but many of the aspects of the service value of acquisitions will apply to all types of libraries.

INTRODUCTION

The acquisition of library materials has been ignored in the literature as a significant point of public service for library patrons. The *ALA Glossary of Library and Information Science* defines public service as "those library activities and operations which entail regular, direct contact between library personnel and library users, in-

---

Stephen Bosch is Acquisitions Librarian for the Humanities and Chris Sugnet is Acquisitions Librarian for the Social Sciences, University of Arizona Library, Tucson, AZ 85721.

cluding circulation services, information services, reprographics services, and others with similar characteristics." Individuals involved with acquisitions may not directly interact with library patrons on a daily basis, yet they do regularly interact with patrons. If viewed on a conceptual level, the impact of acquisitions on a library's collections can establish the parameters which define the fulfillment of a library's mission to its clientele. Most patrons seek a particular information product. Timely acquisition of materials central to the core collection of a particular library greatly enhances the patrons' ability to obtain desired materials. For the purposes of this paper, a general approach will be used to define the procedures involved with the procurement of materials as functions of the acquisitions process. A traditional organization is assumed in which technical and public service functions are performed by individual "specialists." For ease of argument, it is assumed that these processes are performed by a separate, hypothetical "acquisitions unit." In many libraries, the internal organization may divide some of these procedures among a variety of units. Collection development may be responsible for some procedures, while others, such as searching and bibliographic verification, may be centered in a cataloging or bibliographic records unit. The intent of this paper is not to argue that all these points of discussion are the domain of the acquisitions unit only. If other units are responsible for these functions, they may want to investigate the public service aspects of their functions in light of this discussion.

This paper will focus on the service value of acquisitions in an academic library. However, many points will apply to all types of libraries. This discussion concerns the hypothetical potential of the acquisition procedure to be a point of service to the library community. Most libraries will not provide all of these services consistently. Primary acquisitions goals must be met first, then if staffing permits, public service can be provided.

PATRON ORDER REQUESTS

The acquisition of patrons' order requests is one of the basic functions of an acquisitions unit and is also one of the most important aspects of the service value of acquisition activities. Frequently, patrons have unique needs that are not met by materials in the general collection. Often they have seen reviews or references to materials of which library selectors are not aware. Also, these materials may not be provided through approval plans or blanket orders. In order to provide the highest level of service to the public, the acquisition function should be organized to expedite the timely fulfillment of all reasonable patron order requests and to make these materials available to the patron in the shortest amount of time. Most acquisitions units have established procedures to provide a high level of service to patrons ordering materials. Normally, the following points comprise the central service aspects involved in acquiring patrons' requests.

1. Patrons' order requests are treated as priority items during the searching, bibliographic verification, and ordering procedures.
2. Feedback provides the patron with information concerning the progress of the request at the earliest, most convenient point in the process.
3. Information concerning the most appropriate processing of the item (rush cataloging, title held at Loan Desk, etc.) must accompany the title as it moves through the system.
4. Problems involving the order (vendor cancels—order direct, requires prepayment, etc.) are handled quickly, they do not languish until someone can get to them.

All patron requests should be treated on a priority basis during the search and bibliographic verification procedures. It is embarrassing to report back to a patron several months, or years, later on the disposition of the request. Academic libraries could find themselves in this position frequently due to the long periods of time it requires to search, verify and acquire some materials, especially foreign titles. Unless serious staffing shortages exist, patron requests should be processed with the greatest of speed and procedures should be in place that allow the patron to be contacted concerning the progress of the request. This does not imply that as each procedure is completed a patron is notified, but if the patron requested to be informed of an item's availability, a message should be sent either at the time the item is received, cataloged, or on the circulating shelves. If the item is unavailable or must be searched in the out-of-print market, the patrons should be informed. Any major delay in the receipt of an item should be reported to the patron to allow obtaining access to the materials by alternate means.

The service aspect of the acquisition of patron requests may not necessarily involve the actual purchase of materials. Communication about library policy and alternative avenues for obtaining the information may happen as frequently. The size of the materials budget may preclude the purchase of some patron requests. The request may fall outside the scope of the collecting interests of your particular library. There are still several services that can be provided for the patron that will leave a positive impression that an effort has been made to accommodate his needs. Most libraries perform sophisticated searching and verification procedures that patrons are not trained to do. An acquisitions unit can insure that the title requested is not held in the library system and that the bibliographic information (title, ISBN, publisher, price) is correct before returning the request to the patron. This information may assist the patron in obtaining the material elsewhere. The patron may be able to acquire the materials through interlibrary loan, or the item might be available for personal purchase. Even in situations when the actual purchase of an item is unlikely from the outset (due to budgetary, collection development, or other considerations) by searching the request, verifying the bibliographic information, and instructing the patron concerning alternate methods of acquiring the item, an acquisitions unit can provide useful information to patrons.

COLLECTION MANAGEMENT AND RESOURCE SHARING

The prompt acquisition of core materials central to the collections of a particular library greatly enhances patrons' ability to obtain materials on demand. There may be no greater service to a patron than to have the item desired available for use. Acquisitions/collection development is the first step of the process that makes this possible. Obviously, libraries cannot collect everything that may be of interest to everyone they serve. A well coordinated acquisitions/

collection development program should make efficient use of a variety of acquisitions methods (i.e., approval plans, blanket orders, standing orders, bibliographers firm orders, etc.) and should acquire the majority of items required by a library's core collection in a minimum amount of time. By following this policy a patron should have a reasonable amount of success obtaining core materials from the library.

As budgets decrease vis-à-vis the amount of materials available, resource sharing has emerged as another method that can be employed by libraries to improve their ability to provide core materials promptly to their patrons. Resource sharing helps focus collection development activities on those areas that best support the mission of the library. It may seem illogical that the exclusion of some materials from a library's collection can provide a service to its patrons, but by de-emphasizing peripheral areas and strengthening the ability of the library to collect core materials, resource sharing can sometimes do more with less.

AUTOMATED ACQUISITIONS SYSTEMS

Many libraries have automated acquisitions systems. In most situations, some type of system access is provided to the public and it is necessary for the staff in acquisitions to instruct or interpret the system for the public and/or public service units. Prior to automation, the in-process file and other paper files were minimally visible to the public. With automation, the acquisitions function has been translated to a computer. Systems typically display a number of information codes which are now, to some degree, in the public domain. These codes describe a myriad of activities such as serial claim cycles, order types, fund codes, and the current status of an order. The codes are often not meaningful outside the acquisitions unit. Public service units should be trained to provide basic instruction on the interpretation of the local acquisitions system. Even when this has been successfully done, the acquisitions staff frequently work with patrons to interpret complicated records. If serials are involved, the questions revolve around the check-in or bindery records on an automated system, and common information needs include the availability of new issues, information on title changes, and bindery and missing issue status. Some serials receiving units or serials departments staff a serials information point for public access. In other academic settings, it would be common to present public lectures concerning the organization and functioning of the acquisitions system.

Another aspect of automation is the ability of the acquisitions unit to produce significant reports on expenditures or produce significant reports on expenditures or other bibliographic products such as accession lists. Automated systems allow the acquisition staff to produce a wide variety of reports, from general expenditures reports to lists of all serial titles associated with a particular academic department. A report on library expenditures in support of an academic program has become standard in most departments' accreditation reports. Sophisticated routing slips for high demand serials and books can also be produced. Automated systems do enable an acquisitions unit to provide a wide range of services previously impossible to produce in manual systems. However, the level of service provided will be determined by the automated systems limits on function, the amount of staff time available to code orders for data retrieval, and the amount of staff time available to produce the actual products.

INSTRUCTION IN ACQUISITIONS PROCEDURES

The organizational separation of technical and public services sometimes leads to communication problems. In the area of acquisitions/collection development, this can be especially acute as the principals involved are often from both areas. Bibliographers/selectors in charge of collection development typically have public service backgrounds, either as reference librarians, branch managers, or other types of subject specialists. Instruction in acquisitions procedures in needed to minimize problems such as chronic selection of duplicates, or unrealistic expectations of order fulfillment. In academic settings, this instruction may also include interested faculty. To increase the efficiency of selection activities and decrease frustration, the particulars of the acquisitions process must be understood. Active faculty selectors should know what types of materials are supplied automatically by approval plans, blanket orders, or standing orders. Selectors also need to understand the bibliographic verification process necessary to avoid unwanted duplicates. Technical services practices are usually based on perceived public service needs but the connections may not be obvious.

SPECIALIZED REFERENCE SERVICES

Acquisitions and collection development departments offer information services for library clientele with special needs. These queries come either directly from the client, or as a referral from public services, and fall into several categories. Perhaps the most common request is for information about publishers or publishing availability for particular titles (prices, in-print status, etc.). Other varieties of questions run the gamut from vendor (book jobber) reliability and order fulfillment efficiency to methodology that can be employed to purchase esoteric materials, to issues like the relative product quality and reliability of a particular publishing house. Staff involved with the acquisitions function develop a specialized knowledge of the book trade, publishing trends, and the bibliographic control of the book business; this knowledge is an important resource to library patrons as well as local collectors and book stores.

GIFTS AND EXCHANGE OPERATIONS

Many acquisitions departments have sections that deal with gifts, and some also handle exchange programs. The interface with the public is constant, and centers on either receiving donations of books and journals, or in answering questions about these materials. There are requests for information concerning the value of items, the disposal of old books, the probability of inclusion of the donated items into the library's collections, tax laws. Many of these questions are asked of the gifts section directly or come through the reference desk or development officer. All of these types of questions fit into the area most academic libraries define as public service. The gifts staff need to have a familiarity with the book trade, the out-of-print marketplace, and the tax law implications of gifts to not-for-profit organizations. Even when conflict of interest dictates that an actual monetary appraisal can not be offered to the patron, advice in a more general sense can still be valuable. This advice could include referrals to booksellers, appraisers, and to auction houses, or it could include referral to specialized libraries with potential interest in the materials. The Gifts sections also offers help with in-house reference tools such as dealers' catalogs and auction records, and staff should be available so that patrons can complete their gift transaction successfully.

Exchange programs are sometimes the purview of the gifts area in an acquisitions department. Beyond their obvious benefit to the collecting effort, they have the potential for real public service beyond the library. Duplicates are often acquired through the gifts process or during the often complicated purchase of new materials. These duplicates could be exchanged for good will by donating the surplus materials to libraries in third world countries, local prison libraries, or rural school libraries. While not technically an exchange, it serves a *pro bono publico* function that is the truest form of service. The person(s) responsible for the exchange process might be best suited to donate these materials as this task demands understanding and experience with the home institution's procedures for transfer of property.

In any gifts/exchange operation, a strong public services attitude is paramount. The staff deals directly with the public on a daily basis, and in some cases a patron's first contact with the library is with the gifts section. The impression taken away from that experience can have profitable repercussions immediately, or much later on, in terms of good will expressed directly with gifts of materials to the library or in other ways that affect the institution's ability to solicit donors successfully in development campaigns. Gifts sections are in the business of public relations and public service.

IMPLICATIONS FOR THE FUTURE

The automation of the library environment in general, and acquisitions in particular, will enhance on-line access to acquisitions data files and processing information and will facilitate increased information exchange. Perhaps the most obvious development concerns the relation between the "scholars work station" and the acquisitions/collection development unit. In the future it should be possible for systems to filter all received materials and inform users of items of individual interest based on a pre-existent user profile. This could include providing on-line access to table of contents, or providing filters to indexing and abstracting services. Tools normally used in the acquisitions process (book reviews, pre-publication/catalog information, vendor supplied bibliographic information) would be made available on-line for faculty selection. Pre-order files will become interactive, allowing input of order requests or allowing comment on requests already in the system. The acquisitions/collection development process will be extended directly into the patron's office as an information service of the library.

Increased access to data files will enhance information exchange between institutions at the local, regional, and national levels. This will in turn encourage cooperative collection development and facilitate resource sharing. The integration of in-process files, OPACs, on-line cataloging services, and conspectus/collection policy documents will allow institutions to focus on building successful cooperative collection development consortia to improve their ability to cope with the additional costs of electronic formats while continuing to provide access to more traditional forms of publishing.

CONCLUSION

The conventional division of public/technical services function in library organizations does not easily apply to the acquisitions unit. Acquisitions bridges the gap between traditional public service and the hidden processes of technical service. By providing information directly to patrons, both on a need to know basis and through organized instructional efforts, the acquisitions staff participate in the overall provision of service to library clientele. In addition to direct service to the public, they also indirectly serve library clientele by managing a library's resources to maximize the amount of information available to patrons. An effective acquisitions program must be composed of aspects of public services (reference service, faculty liaison, public instruction) and aspects of technical services to be truly successful.

Vendor Performance Evaluation
as a Model
for Evaluating Acquisitions

Donna Alsbury

SUMMARY. While the goals of an acquisitions department may not be the same as those of a library materials vendor, they share similar objectives. An acquisitions department must place orders for as many requests as possible, obtain items quickly and economically, and provide additional information through the maintenance of statistics and records. To be successful vendors must fill a reasonable percentage of orders quickly and at a competitive price while providing additional customer services. If acquisitions and vendors do share similar objectives, can the criteria used to evaluate vendor performance be applied to the evaluation of acquisitions functions? This article will address the question by reviewing guides to and studies of vendor performance in an attempt to determine which criteria could be applicable to the evaluation of acquisitions.

INTRODUCTION

Given an adequate, motivated, and well-trained staff, an acquisitions department might purchase materials from the fastest source, for the cheapest price, and might eventually locate a source for almost all requested items. This is, of course, while maintaining records and statistics which can provide a response to any question asked or any analysis needed.

Finding the "perfect" vendor would certainly help. Unfortunately there is no perfect vendor for any library. Through vendor

---

Donna Alsbury is User Services Librarian for Acquisitions and Serials Control at Florida Center for Library Automation, 2002 NW 13th Street, Suite 320, Gainesville, FL 32611.

performance studies, libraries have attempted to identify the best
vendors—those who provide the highest fulfillment rate, fastest delivery speed, greatest discount, and best service.[1] It is also doubtful
that there is a "perfect" acquisitions department. Examination and
analysis of organizational structure, procedures, and personnel can
help to identify strengths and weaknesses within the department.
Since both acquisitions and dealer effectiveness are judged on the
ability to provide materials for the library, several common vendor
evaluation techniques could be applied to the library acquisitions
process.

A review of the literature on vendor performance indicates that
there are four factors most frequently considered when evaluating a
vendor—fulfillment rate, speed, discount, and service. By examining the methods used to evaluate vendors on each of these factors,
techniques may be identified which can be applied to the measurement of acquisitions effectiveness. In addition, some design considerations in a well constructed vendor study are also applicable to the
study of acquisitions operations.

MOTIVATION FOR EVALUATION

Vendor selection is often based on tradition or assumption. Dis-
satisfaction with a current vendor, reduced buying power, or the
desire to base decisions on more objective criteria can lead to a
formal evaluation of vendor performance. The results put libraries
in a better position to communicate with suppliers about needed
improvements in service and can serve as justification for dropping
a vendor. The identification of each vendor's strengths and weaknesses also helps in formulating guidelines that can be used in making specific ordering decisions.

While vendor studies normally compare the performance of two
or more vendors, comparisons between acquisitions departments in
different libraries are less likely. Although it is common practice for
librarians to share statistics and information about policies and procedures, no two departments are alike. The type, size, organization,
and governance of each library makes it difficult to equate even
commonly used measurements. Even specific definitions may be
interpreted differently. For example, the Board of Regents of the

State University System of Florida used the Washington Formula to allocate funds to each of the nine universities for materials purchases. One of the factors used in the formula was unit cost. "Units" were specifically defined, yet somehow each library managed to interpret the definitions in a way that suited their specific circumstances.

Therefore, rather than comparing different libraries, an acquisitions evaluation should more likely involve a comparison between level of activity during different time periods, the varying effects of diverse procedures, or the relative productivity of individual employees. Most acquisitions departments keep various types of statistics which are used to document historical performance and make year-to-year comparisons. In many cases, however, the criteria used to gather the statistics will change each year and the interpretation of the statistics may be rudimentary. Some vendor studies can be similarly criticized.

The consequences of automation or a change in departmental organization or procedures can be assessed by comparing productivity both before and after the change is made. A vendor study can document the effects of change. Baumann, for example, mentions the impact of a dealer going out of business, a change in a dealer's back-order procedures, and the effect of vendor automation on fulfillment rates.[2] While these observations are only the by-product of a vendor study, an acquisitions department can intentionally design studies to assess the consequences of internal changes.

The results of a performance evaluation can also be used as feedback to apprise staff members within the department of their individual or collective effectiveness just as the results of a vendor study are often used to talk to vendors about improving service.

Evaluation Design Issues

There is no single means for evaluating vendor performance. Reported methods range from the review of data generated by an automated acquisitions system[3] to the sophisticated statistical analysis of the results of a controlled evaluation project.[4] There is also no single method for evaluating acquisitions, just the necessity for using relevant, structured, and unbiased techniques. While I am not suggesting that an "acquisitions performance study" be undertaken, certain common criteria used in vendor performance studies may be applicable to the evaluation of acquisitions.

Vendor performance evaluations may be considered a luxury when the workload is heavy. Thus descriptions of most studies report that they were designed to create minimal interruption of normal processes. Similarly, the analysis of acquisitions activities assumes a low priority when the workload is heavy, so minimal disruption of workflow must be considered when designing acquisitions evaluations.

No study can include every aspect of vendor or of acquisitions performance. The areas chosen for evaluation should reflect the priorities of the library and the greatest weight should be given to those factors considered most important. When the budget is extremely limited, a vendor's discount may be more significant than the time taken to receive material. In an acquisitions department, if the law requires prompt payment, processing invoices may be more important than processing books.

A comparative evaluation—whether it be a comparison of vendors, historical performance, procedures, or personnel—must insure that the comparison includes similar samples. The ideal vendor study involves the sending of duplicate orders to various vendors at the same time. This is not practical in most libraries. Instead, a vendor study must be designed to insure that a comparable sample of orders is sent to each vendor. The same is true in acquisitions evaluation. Any comparative evaluation of acquisitions functions must be based on similar samples. Comparing the productivity of the staff member who searches in-print, English-language requests to the productivity of the staff member who searches out-of-print or foreign-language orders is an invalid comparison.

Most studies rate dealers based on a cross-section of orders. Others also isolate more specific categories of materials to determine if there are advantages to using specialized dealers. For example, as part of Barker's study, orders for art books, reprints, English-language Canadian titles, and U.S. documents were assigned to an appropriate specialized dealer or to a general-purpose vendor from a control group.[5] (In this particular instance, the study indicated that the specialized dealers were generally no more effective than the general purpose vendor.) Since acquisitions departments may be structured to take advantage of the individual aptitudes of staff members, such as subject background or foreign-language skill, it may be appropriate to conduct a similar study to determine if, for example, there is added efficiency in having a music major search order requests for scores.

Fulfillment

Fulfillment rate is a factor considered in most vendor evaluations. Records are kept of the number of orders placed with a vendor and the percentage of the orders which are supplied. All orders may be included, as well as specifically selected subsets of orders, such as those with publishers not verified in *Books in Print*.

As with vendors, acquisitions departments are constantly judged on their ability to obtain requested materials. While it is important to get items quickly and at the best price, the main objective is to *get* them. For a library, overall fulfillment rates will include not only the number of orders received but also the percent of requests for items that result in the placement of an order.

A vendor study can be used to monitor the number of orders filled and an internal study can be used to monitor the number of orders placed. Searching order requests and placing orders are roughly equivalent to vendor fulfillment rates and might be examined in a similar manner. Every request could be included in an overall measure and specific categories (formats, subjects, languages, etc.) might be isolated to document changes in the type of requests submitted.

Even the best vendors are unable to fill all orders. Some titles are out-of-print, are available only from the publisher, or are not yet published. Likewise, not all order requests result in the placement of an order. Before an order is placed, a requested title may be identified as out-of-print, not yet published, or the duplicate of an item already owned by the library. A change in the proportion of orders placed could be a reflection of acquisitions efficiency or might, just as easily, be the result of incomplete or inaccurate information contained in the request and reflect on the abilities of those *making* the requests. These circumstances must be taken into consideration when evaluating fulfillment statistics.

There are instances when a vendor might erroneously report items as out-of-print or otherwise unavailable. Vendors may also fail to fill orders for available items because of poor follow-up with publishers. Bracken and Calhoun reported that of 274 orders left unfilled by their major vendor and subsequently mailed to six competing dealers, 38% were filled within ten weeks and 60% were filled within twenty weeks.[6] As a result of doubts about the credibility of their dealer's reports, a library in another study sent orders cancelled by the dealer directly to publishers.[7] The publishers filled a majority of the orders. Likewise, library orders may not be placed (or may be placed incorrectly) because of incomplete or erroneous searching. In an acquisitions department, a study could be designed in which requests that were unsuccessfully or incorrectly searched would be given to a higher-level staff member who would repeat the search, including additional verification tools as needed. The results could be used to determine if routine re-searching is desirable or to identify staff who need to improve performance.

Techniques used to evaluate fulfillment are not suited to the acquisitions functions of receiving, paying, and record keeping. There is an assumption that every order filled (except those lost in transit) will be processed, that each invoice will be paid, and that every transaction will be recorded. Ninety percent might be an acceptable fulfillment rate for a vendor, but any department that could account for only 90% of the items shipped would quickly encounter serious problems.

Speed

Acquisitions tasks must also be completed quickly. When a title is requested, the person making the request often expects the item to be on the shelf yesterday. Choosing a vendor that can supply items promptly can greatly enhance a library's ability to satisfy its patrons, so delivery speed is an important consideration in vendor performance studies.

In vendor studies, delivery speed is most often measured by computing the average time between the mailing of orders and the arrival of materials. The results provide a means for an overall comparison of delivery speed. In an example included in study by Kim, average delivery time for 32 duplicate titles ordered directly from the publishers and from 4 dealers ranged from 18.2 days for the publisher to 53 days for one of the dealers.[8]

A more comprehensive analysis of delivery speed may include median turn-around time or fulfillment percentage at pre-determined time intervals (e.g., 0-30 days). These measures provide additional means for analysis and help in drawing conclusions. For example, in Kim's study, three of the four vendors had similar average delivery times (31.5 days, 35.3 days, and 38.4 days), but their fulfillment patterns varied greatly. The dealer with the fastest average speed had supplied approximately 66% of the titles within three weeks. At the same time, the second dealer had supplied only 3% (1 title) and the third had supplied none. By the sixth week, however, both the second and third vendors had surpassed the first in fulfillment rate. As a result, Kim concluded that the first, a large dealer, would be most appropriate for high demand items normally kept in stock. The other two dealers were smaller and apparently were more successful in obtaining unstocked titles from the publishers.[9]

Speed in performing acquisitions activities is also commonly reported as a mean. It would be significant to know that, for example, in 1990 the average time needed to place a requested order was 10 days but in 1989 the average time was only five days. An assumption might be made that overall productivity had dropped. It is possible, however, that although the average time doubled from 1989 to 1990, the median time decreased and that in 1990, 100% of requests were ordered within a week while in 1989, only 50% had been ordered. This would indicate that while the speed at which most requests were being processed had increased, some were being processed very slowly, possibly due to an increase in the number of more difficult requests.

Tests of order speed can also be used to identify exceptions not covered by standard procedures, to evaluate the effects of new procedures, and to judge employee performance. Using the example above, a review of the orders which took longest to process might reveal that they were for foreign-language titles and that normal procedures did not include verification in foreign equivalents to

Books in Print. After a change in procedures to include these tools, the effect (or lack of effect) could be documented by repeating the analysis. Using the same example, it might be discovered that one staff member was responsible for the orders that took the longest to process. A review of the orders could help to determine whether the staff member was inefficient or just dealing with more problematic orders. Similarly, if the performance speed of individual staff members is being compared, median or percentage analysis can help in ascertaining the reasons for less than average productivity. Speed is a criterion on which many acquisitions functions can be evaluated. While the turn-around time between the receipt of order requests and the placement of orders most closely parallels vendor delivery speed, the time taken to unpack and check shipments, to process materials, and to pay invoices can be evaluated using the same methods.

Discount

An acquisitions department must obtain materials at the lowest possible price. Performance studies can be used to discover which vendors provide the best discounts and lowest service charges. It is fairly simple to determine the discounts given by suppliers. Discount rates are usually listed on invoices and average discounts are not difficult to calculate. The same is true for postage and handling charges. In a vendor study, comparisons can be made between the order price (based on BIP, catalogs, reviews, etc.), the list price, the discounted price, and the actual price paid.

Acquisitions departments do not give discounts or charge postage and handling, so the methods used to determine the cost of materials cannot be applied in calculating the cost of obtaining the materials. However, the results of a traditional production cost analysis can be used in conjunction with the results of a vendor performance study to establish the "real" cost of materials. A vendor study might show that one dealer provides the best discount, but because it is more expensive to obtain and process materials from that dealer, the good discount may be negated.

Service

It is difficult to quantify and compare vendors' services so most libraries base their appraisals of dealer service on staff impressions. In fact, the *Guide to Performance Evaluation of Library Materials Vendors* lists service elements as "Qualitative Assessment" as opposed to "Quantitative Measures," which include fulfillment rate, discount, and turn-around time.[10] Invoice format, prompt status reporting, and a good return policy do not lend themselves to numeric analysis.

It is even more difficult to quantify the service aspects of acquisitions. The first difficulty is in the identification of what constitutes "service" in a technical services department. Lack of errors? Quickly answering questions as to the status of order requests? Providing accurate financial or operational statistics on a regular basis? Providing ad hoc reports to library management immediately upon request?

Some reported methods for analyzing vendors' service included combining staff interviews with counting errors, claims, and reports[11] and assigning specified numbers of points to various service criteria.[12] Even if appropriate acquisitions activities could be identified as service functions, it would be difficult to apply these methods to an assessment of the department as a whole.

Evaluation of acquisitions service activities are more likely to involve the performance evaluation of individual employees. But the criteria and methods used in a personnel evaluation are normally established by the library or the parent institution and may have little to do with acquisitions.

CONCLUSION

Vendors are in business to make money, libraries are not. Nevertheless, they do share the common objective of providing materials for library users and share common concerns about fulfillment, speed, discount (cost), and quality of service. Both vendors and acquisitions departments can be evaluated on those factors and, in some instances, similar evaluative techniques can be used, particularly in the areas of fulfillment and speed. If the assessment of acquisitions functions in a library has historically been based on assumption and subjective impression, the design of a well constructed vendor performance study can serve as a model for a more structured, objective assessment.

Still, acquisitions department efficiency and effectiveness is dependent on good vendors. When a successful vendor has been identified, an acquisitions administrator may find it worthwhile to explore the techniques used by the vendor and consider whether similar techniques could be used to improve acquisitions procedures. In the final analysis, one of the most significant ways to evaluate an acquisitions department may be on the ability to evaluate and learn from its vendors.

REFERENCES

1. Annotated bibliographies of works on vendor evaluation are contained in: American Library Association. Collection Management and Development Committee and Acquisitions Committee, *Guide to Performance Evaluation of Library Materials Vendors* (Chicago: American Library Association, 1988), 15-20; and Association for Higher Education of North Texas. Vendor Study Group, "Vendor Evaluation: A Selected Annotated Bibliography, 1955-1987," *Library Acquisitions: Practice & Theory* 12 (1988):17-28.

2. Baumann, Susan, "An Extended Application of Davis' 'Model for a Vendor Study,'" *Library Acquisitions: Practice & Theory* 9 (1985):317-329.

3. Uden, Janet, "Financial Reporting and Vendor Performance: A Case Study," *Journal of Library Automation* 13 (September 1980): 191-195.

4. Cooper, Michael D., "Modeling Arrival Patterns of Library Book Orders," *Library & Information Science Research* 10 (1988): 237-255. Analysis based on the study reported in: Barker, Joseph W., "Random Vendor Assignment in Vendor Performance Evaluation," *Library Acquisitions: Practice & Theory* 10 (1986):265-280.

5. Barker, 273.

6. Bracken, James K. and John C. Calhoun, "Profiling Vendor Performance," *Library Resources & Technical Services* 28 (April/June 1984):123.

7. Safran, Franciska, "Defensive Ordering," *Library Acquisitions: Practice & Theory* 3 (1979):6. One hundred percent of the titles reported as "OP" and 65% reported as "OS," "TOS," or "POS" were received. Seventy five percent of the "NYP" titles were received within 60 days. Approximately 90% of automatic cancellations were also received.

8. Kim, Ung Chon, "Purchasing Books from Publishers and Wholesalers," *Library Resources & Technical Services* 19 (Spring 1975):136-143.

9. Kim, 142-143.

10. ALA, 4-7.

11. Stokley, Sandra L. and Marion T. Reed, "A Study of Performance of Five Book Dealers Used by Louisiana State University Library," *Library Resources & Technical Services* 22 (Spring 1978):117-125.

12. Davis, Mary Byrd, "Model for a Vendor Study in a Manual or Semi-Automated Acquisitions System," *Library Acquisitions: Practice & Theory* 3 (1979):53-60.

Evaluation Under the Gun: Not Necessarily Inferior

Miriam Palm
Vicky Reich

SUMMARY. When we think of "evaluation," it is as a thoughtful, planned process, performed deliberately and thoroughly, and bringing all relevant facts and opinions to bear. In the academic library environment in particular, we favor evaluation by consensus, consulting the widest possible range of interested and affected constituencies. Situations can arise, however, which preclude a reasoned and leisurely pace; reacting to a crisis can mandate a "gut level" assessment, and force evaluation and the resulting decisions into a very short timeframe. As we learned at Stanford this past year, such "quick and dirty" evaluation does not necessarily yield inferior results.

WHEN THE EARTH MOVED

Nearly everyone has heard about the October 17, 1989 earthquake in Northern California, which affected Stanford University by virtue of its location and condition. Another crisis, of a different nature but perhaps with equally long-term effects, also had its impact on Stanford during the past year: a directive to reduce the University operating budget to offset a projected deficit of $22 million. Although one's first impression might be that these are very different crises, we found it fascinating to compare the way the Stanford University Libraries, in particular the Serials and Acquisitions Departments, reacted to each. What we learned was that many of the

---

Miriam Palm is Senior Acquisitions Librarian and Vicky Reich is Acquisitions Chief at Stanford University Libraries, Stanford, CA 94305.

"seat of the pants" evaluations and techniques used in response to the quake were applicable to our second "disaster" as well.

EARTHQUAKE RECOVERY

Stanford University, along with a significant part of the San Francisco Bay Area and beyond, was abruptly brought to a halt at 5:04 p.m. on Tuesday, October 17, by a 7.1 earthquake on the Loma Prieta portion of the San Andreas fault. When the earthquake occurred, few staff were in the central Green Library facility, and those who were, were fortunate to suffer only minor injuries. Green Library along with all other campus buildings remained closed the following day so that engineers could perform initial estimates of the severity of the damage. Green Library consists of a West Wing constructed in 1919 and an East Wing constructed in 1979; the former houses the Technical Services operation on the first floor.

The engineers' initial assessment of the older West Wing was conservatively pessimistic: possible major structural damage and a great deal of visible but possibly superficial damage resulted in a decision to keep this part of the building closed. This conclusion resulted in the need to relocate immediately 150 staff in Technical Services. Staff were asked to report to work if possible on Thursday, October 19, where they were assigned to teams to return to adjacent shelving the many items knocked to the floor in aisles in the East Wing. After the aisles were cleared, a major shelf-reading project was mounted to put the materials back in proper order: all willing hands were welcomed to participate in this project.

By the following week, further study indicated that Green West was structurally safe on the first floor and that reoccupancy would be likely in a month or so. Managers quickly evaluated the options and decided to return as many functions to a semblance of normal activity as possible. One of the first units to resume "normal" operations was serials check-in, in part as a response to the large volumes of third class mail piling up in the central receiving unit. Managers wearing hard hats entered the closed building to retrieve the manual serials holdings and payments file, cataloging worksheets awaiting keying into RLIN, invoices awaiting payment, and other essential items needed to start up operations. By October 25, Serials had set up business in a circulation sort room in the East Wing, and current receipts began to flow to their shelving locations. Invoice processing also resumed, and within another week when the backlog of mail receipts was cleared, claiming of missing issues as well.

Acquisitions Department staff, dependent on the use of RLIN for most of their basic functions, were able to return to order request processing by sharing RLIN terminals with their East Wing colleagues in collection development and interlibrary loan, and the Meyer Undergraduate Library. At first, they concentrated on "rush" and priority orders, gradually handling all other types as well. By November 1, the Receipts unit was attending to the backlog of unopened packages, concentrating on those identified as firm orders, and sorting them by supplier and by estimated date of receipt (oldest material first). Several major suppliers were contacted and asked to hold shipments for a few weeks. Approval plan processing was postponed until a temporary review area on book trucks could be organized. Processing of monographs on exchange was temporarily suspended, as was all gifts processing. Use of electronic mail was encouraged to request urgently needed items which might be in process. Electronic mail was vital for communication during this time of relocation since e-mail addresses remained constant. Daily changes in phone numbers, hours of operation and location of work units were transmitted via e-mail.

Budget "Repositioning"

The University budget reduction efforts were announced in early February 1990. By mid-February, a formal structure with a central "steering committee" was announced, and information about the process began to flow downward to units such as the Libraries. In early March, units were given percentage targets for reductions and asked to look at administrative structures and processes, with a goal of "keeping the University properly proportioned between academic and non-academic functions."

The University Libraries' initial target was a 20% cut, representing a figure of $1,043,000 within Technical Services. Department managers had two weeks to work with the Director of Technical Services to evaluate options and first estimate, and then define, exactly what a cut of this magnitude would mean to the operation. Lengthy discussions ensued before proposed cuts were offered to a Library-wide committee, which in turn presented a menu of scenarios, describing the impact of such cuts on the Libraries' program, to the University steering committee on March 30. After review by that committee, the Library was asked on April 11 to revise its proposals to meet a 16% target, and this plan was submitted on May 18. All cuts up to 13% have been accepted, and the final 3% will be identified after further study.

Assessment Out of Necessity

These two situations are interesting to compare and contrast. Both are examples of "management in crisis," yet they can be distinguished by the way decisions were made, the way communication took place, the ways staff reacted, and the values that were placed on work priorities. During the earthquake, all work stopped; the initial concern was the staff's safety, after which we began to reconstruct the most vital pieces of our operation from the ground up. Repositioning involved a conceptual reorganization: taking a fully functional operation apart, making rapid decisions about what parts of it were most essential, and agreeing to give up less essential functions.

How Decisions Were Made

The earthquake forced us to look at what was really important and what could be set aside on a temporary basis. We all felt free to try out ideas, since we had nothing to lose; risk-taking became more accepted than under normal circumstances. Managers were very open with each other and with their staffs about what was possible and what would have to be given up. Because we were starting with nothing, every accomplishment or problem solved gave us a positive feeling, and invigorated us with a sense of purpose. Although managers were making many of the decisions, they relied upon staff to transform the plans into realities.

Because we did not know when we would be able to return to our normal work space, we planned for the worst contingency, and reestablished the most crucial operations rather than postponing decisions. We accepted the fact that communications with service points were impaired, and concentrated on moving the most bulky and most critical items on their way. We did not stop to document decisions, but invested our energies in implementing them.

Many of the techniques we used during the earthquake, and the closeness that Technical Services managers developed while communicating with each other and reaching compromises, served us well during the budget repositioning discussions. The process itself was quite different: instructions and deadlines with which we were expected to comply came down from upper levels of the University. The end goal, saving a particular dollar amount, was known. Each unit brought initial "offerings" which represented that unit's share of the cut, but we evaluated and ranked each offering as we considered them, and rejected some as having consequences we could not accept. Because we were preparing proposals for possible cuts rather than making final decisions, the information was highly confidential and we were unable to test our ideas on staff, a mode unusual for Stanford. We had to rely on only each other's judgment to a major extent.

Although meetings were usually structured and task-oriented, we continued to benefit from our closeness during discussions of programs to be cut; individual points of view were set aside to the greatest possible extent. No ideas were deemed "too crazy" for the situation, and the sense of working as a team helped counter the negative effects of making major programmatic cuts. We all felt like we were in it together.

Style and Levels of Communication

Following the *earthquake*, it was important to communicate what was known quickly, to share information and to obviate panic; while most information was transmitted "top down" for efficiency, it was passed along as soon as it was received, giving everyone the same news within a short period of time. Confidence that all reliable information was being shared fostered cooperation and helpfulness among all staff; any vestiges of territoriality quickly dissipated. As staff were scattered around the Libraries, daily meetings at a regular place and time brought people back together to share their experiences and keep in touch with co-workers.

Managers camped out in the Directors' Office, meeting with each other several times daily and checking in more frequently; these meetings resulted in decisions which were implemented by reporting back to all-staff meetings. The managers' meetings also served as emotional steam valves for us; we frequently broke into laughter or (less frequently) tears, to release the tension we all felt. The Director's secretary manned the "communications center," taking telephone messages for all Technical Services staff; dozens of little yellow message slips ringed the frame of the Director's door during these weeks. Everyone had the sense that we all were working together to re-establish normal operations as best we could.

Because of the confidential nature of the "*repositioning*" discussions, staff could be told only about the process we were following; they had to trust their managers, and it was difficult to ask them to "buy into" the process. There was a much greater need to filter information and share things selectively; what was released was well-considered before it was shared. Information about process was released through a series of memoranda from both the central steering committee and the Libraries' own committee. Managers also gave status reports at department and division-wide open meetings, where staff were given the opportunity to ask questions; however, a frequent response to their questions was "I don't know."

Responses of Line Staff

Managers were not the only ones evaluating these situations as a basis for decisions regarding behaviors and priorities. The *earthquake* reduced everyone to a common denominator, all facing the same set of problems such as "how will I get to work, and what will there be for me to do when I get there?" After safety issues had been resolved, the next issues addressed were the basics required to resume "normal" work as much as possible. While managers were dealing with matters of logistics (where to put people; where to set up temporary shop for units; how to recapture resources unavailable to us in the closed building), staff provided key information about what equipment and supplies were critical to starting work again, and what they could do without. It was gratifying to find that people quickly could draw distinctions between vital needs and less important items, and were extremely conservative about how little they needed. As an example, the entire Serials Department (25 people) was relocated to a single, large circulation sorting room, in which staff made use of equipment in place (large tables, a few desks, and shelving on the walls) to simulate their usual working environment. The Acquisitions Department worked in a reading area on the third floor of the stacks with several large tables and carrels; most of their operations were performed via booktrucks as staff cruised the building in search of RLIN terminals in public services and collection development areas. Serials staff shared a single telephone line; Acquisitions was completely without telephone access, yet staff were extremely sanguine about these conditions throughout the entire course of their "exodus" of 17 working days.

Getting back to "normal" work helped to dispel the sense of displacement and loss that all staff naturally felt. The ability to communicate all news as soon as it was known helped everyone pull together and maintain a spirit of optimism even when it appeared we might be displaced for a long time. Learning that we would be able to reoccupy the first floor of the damaged building was met with mixed reactions, as many people were concerned about the building's safety (all upper floors remain closed to this day), but others enjoyed the adventure and departure from routine. Communication about this matter was enhanced by arranging meetings with the engineers who had inspected the building; hearing their direct responses to questions contributed greatly to dispelling anxiety about moving back into the damaged wing.

On November 9, the date of our reoccupation, an all-staff project to clean up the plaster dust which had settled onto every flat surface, and to tidy up individual work areas, helped reacclimatize us to our somewhat altered surroundings. Several Technical Services units displaced from damaged portions of the building were squeezed into "least used" parts of the floor that suddenly had become "prime real estate," and the official shelf list was relocated into the East Wing in the public catalog area. All staff were encouraged to make suggestions about improvements to the work environment to overcome the feeling of loss, and these were acted upon as quickly as was feasible: installing additional shelving and acquiring better lighting were but two suggestions we were able to meet. As time passed and major aftershocks subsided, the sense of stress gradually dissipated and attention turned to digging out from the backlogs of work that had accumulated.

The initial announcement of *"repositioning"* alarmed most of the staff, but when there was no immediate effect of the announcement, most people went about their business without feeling overstressed. Because the Library Materials Budget was not considered within the scope of the initial 20% cut, Technical Services staff may have felt a bit more "protected," as they assumed with justification that their role in expending that budget was not insignificant. They were kept informed about the process but not the content of what was being examined, although many of them were able to make educated guesses about what was under scrutiny. A certain sense of "they can't do this to us," and a denial that the Libraries provide administrative rather than direct academic support to the central mission of the University, also kept anxiety at a relatively low level. Only when the final 16% cuts were announced, and realization that actual positions were targeted, did anger and resentment begin to surface.

EVALUATION OF WORK PRIORITIES

Priorities established after the earthquake were determined by very pragmatic considerations, such as keeping people busy with useful work, and preventing the ongoing receipt of mail shipments from becoming totally out of control. One major constraint was access to the RLIN processing system, upon which many units were heavily dependent. We were without access to over 50 terminals in the closed building, and had to make the best use of those located elsewhere. Other Library units which were not displaced were extremely generous in sharing their access, and we acted upon items we might otherwise lose, such as monograph orders and serials claims, as a high priority. Knowing what serials issues had arrived by checking them in assisted both the claiming work and the continuing mail problems. Monographic receipts, however, could be stored and worked off at a slower pace, as could monographic in-

voices. Dealing with non-urgent problems and questions was postponed while normal processing took precedence.

Our approach to the budget reduction target was to determine
what the minimum was we could live with: which components of
our operations were basic "core" programs, and which were em-
bellishments which had become "essential" over time. We also
considered the level and amount of resources needed to perform a
function, in comparison with the "payoff" or results. Some examples of things we discussed were:

1. What number of claims sent for missing serial issues resulted
   in what percentage of those issues being received? Were third
   claims really effective in acquiring a significant portion of otherwise missing material?
2. Could work currently done by highly paid experts be distributed among staff at lower classification levels? Were we really
   using these "experts" most effectively?
3. Could some processing of standard LC copy be handled in
   Acquisitions by receiving staff, rather than being routed and
   rehandled by admittedly more expert staff in Cataloging?
4. Were we willing to forfeit some of our built-in flexibility to
   handle projects, large gifts, and other unanticipated increases
   in workload, by cutting out nearly all of our "slack?"
5. Could we accept a lower quality record at the point of acquisition, rather than investing time in seeking out the "best copy"
   at that point in the process?

As we discussed these and many other ideas, we became fully
aware that to do the same amount of work with fewer staff, we
would have to accept a lower quality and more standardized product, less "special handling," and less flexibility to respond to particular needs. Over the years, both managers and staff have come to
take a great deal of pride in their ability to cater to these factors, and
giving them up will come at some emotional cost. However, some
of the changes we have agreed to are ideas we have had in mind for
some time and which repositioning is enabling us to try.

In sharing ideas and feelings with each other, the group of managers who made the decisions gained a higher level of confidence

that the right decisions were being made, despite a definite level of discomfort which was present as we made them. We kept each other from feeling overly uncomfortable, in part because we were trading functions and expertise across our departments and gaining a better understanding of the entire operation through our deliberations. We questioned each other and reasoned through the process even when we knew the results would repudiate some long-standing Stanford traditions, and would require extremely deft "salesmanship" to persuade the staff performing the work that the shortcuts were at the very least worth trying. One area which is hard for us to judge objectively is the trimming of our management structure: while we kept most unit managers in place, we gave up more than one-third of our department level managers, and we have yet to know the full effect of this change.

When forced to abandon our tradition, respected methods of evaluating processes and priorities, we at Stanford learned an important first-hand lesson this past year: that when placed in difficult situations, we can make valid and useful decisions, with limited resources available to us, in compressed periods of time. These decisions, made with a minimum of documentation, bureaucracy and consulting, were eased by the collegial closeness of a core group of managers, and reinforced to each of us the benefits of helping and relying on others around us in a crisis. We expect many aspects of this new way of "doing business" to remain the norm for us — at least for some time to come.

EVALUATING THE COLLECTORS AND ACQUIRERS

Performance Evaluation of Collection Development and Acquisitions Librarians

E. Anne Edwards

SUMMARY. Collection development and acquisitions activities are of great and critical importance to libraries. Likewise, performance evaluations in libraries are deemed to be critical; a great deal of time, energy, and emotion is spent on this library activity. Although such importance is attached to both collection development/acquisitions activities and personnel evaluations, little has been written on the link between the two; how to evaluate effectively those with collection development and acquisitions responsibilities. There is a continuing need for thoughtful and constructive evaluation of those who select, acquire, and manage library collections. These evaluations need to be geared to the responsibilities and expectations of such individuals, rather than to the librarians' general performance.

E. Anne Edwards is Associate Dean of Access Services, University of Alabama Libraries, Box 870266, Tuscaloosa, AL 35487-0266. She holds the MLS from the University of Western Ontario and an MA in Italian Studies from Aberdeen University, Scotland.

INTRODUCTION

Librarians are no strangers to personnel performance evaluation as is evidenced by the wealth of material in this area. Articles abound with topics such as how to evaluate personnel, legal aspects of evaluation, promotion and tenure evaluations, performance standards, types of evaluations, and goals and objectives.[1,2,3] Many of these articles, however, concentrate on the evaluation of librarians as members of an organization, and not in relation to the particular responsibilities of their positions. Evaluation forms may reflect the emphasis on librarians as members of the organization through the inclusion of questions concerning the librarians' progress in terms of general performance, collegiality, professionalism, and so on. It is more difficult to find evaluation forms that are geared specifically to the individual duties and responsibilities of a librarian, such as the teaching ability of a bibliographic instruction librarian, or a reference librarian's knowledge of particular reference tools. If these areas are covered at all, they may be included in a comments section, where no parameters are specified. Thus the supervisor is required to decide whether to devote attention to performance of specific duties, and if so, in how much detail. Questions on specific duties, responsibilities, and skills are more likely to be asked in the evaluation process for support staff, where the supervisor is asked to indicate, for example, the level of accuracy in posting of invoices, word processing, shelving, or copy cataloging.

The literature teems with information on evaluation by librarians of services, collections, vendors, approval plans, and other library activities, but there appears to be a dearth of references to evaluation of specific duties and responsibilities of librarians. In a field where we place so much emphasis on service, and profess a desire to strive for excellence in that service, it is surprising that there has been little effort made to focus on the level of performance of the librarians providing the service. It is quite possible to set up an evaluation system that assesses the performance of librarians according to the responsibilities of their positions, yet it seems that there are few examples of such a system. There is some encouragement in a chapter by Maxine Reneker and Virginia Steel, where they cover all aspects of performance appraisal and indicate that there is evidence of some progress in relating performance evaluation to specific responsibilities.[4]

In the case of collection development and acquisitions librarians, placing our emphasis on evaluation of their general library performance is problematic, since "the work of selecting and procuring library materials is critical to all types of libraries."[5] It would seem to be sensible and of crucial importance to evaluate the performance of the specific duties of those we hire in collection development and acquisitions, especially given that these librarians frequently hold full or partial responsibility for the library materials budget.

DEFINITIONS

For the sake of clarity, I shall use a definition of collection development as the responsibility for building and maintaining the collections through materials selection, collection analysis, de-selection, materials budget allocation, and acquisitions as the technical responsibility of acquiring materials for the collections, through order and receipt. Collection development and acquisitions librarians may have similar responsibilities, and their duties may, and probably should, overlap. They should certainly work cooperatively, even if their duties are clearly separate.

PERFORMANCE EVALUATIONS

Traditionally, evaluations have been dreaded or at best considered a necessary evil, and they certainly absorb a seemingly inordinate amount of time. Those who prepare and those who receive them may view the process simply as an onerous task to be performed at regular intervals. Hours are spent agonizing over phraseology, fairness, impact, objectivity, and other concerns before the process is completed. Librarians in academic settings may even feel that regular evaluation is unnecessary once tenure is attained. In spite of these apprehensive and somewhat negative approaches there are many reasons to view performance evaluation as an important and positive feature of the organizational structure. For example, evaluations may be used as the basis for salary increases, in which case it is sensible and necessary to ensure that the evaluation is carefully prepared. It must be balanced, detailed, specific, and provide for constructive direction.

Planning in advance for performance evaluation is essential to a constructive and useful process. Of primary importance is a clear understanding by both the supervisor and the librarian regarding responsibilities and expectations. Attainable goals and objectives should be drafted, based on the specific responsibilities of the librarian involved.

Many questions need to be discussed and answered before goals are established. What goals are conducive to quantitative assessment? Which ones are purely qualitative? For example, one goal for a collection development librarian might be to expend or encumber certain percentages of the budget by certain dates during the fiscal year. This would be an appropriate goal for a beginning librarian, or one who has experienced difficulty in meeting deadlines, but it might be less important for a librarian who has consistently demonstrated success in this area of responsibility. Goals must be based on the areas where improvements on the part of the librarian are warranted, and on the needs of the organization. Accountability, especially where fiscal responsibilities are concerned, is in the best interest of both parties.

Opportunities for improvement through training or development, such as workshops, continuing education and credit classes, or attendance at special conferences should be identified so that librarians can reach their goals. Also, there needs to be regular and constructive communication between the supervisor and the librarian in an effort to relieve the process of its traditionally aversive nature.

The clarification of responsibilities and expectations in advance of the evaluation serves another purpose in instances where the supervisor of the collection development or acquisitions librarian may not have detailed knowledge of the work involved. The librarian may report to a director or department head responsible for a variety of library functions. Without the aid of adequately prepared goals, the supervisor may not be able to evaluate the librarian's performance fairly and effectively.

RESPONSIBILITIES AND EXPECTATIONS

What do collection development and acquisitions librarians do? What should they know? How should they act? Several articles in the literature give examples of the qualities that should be found in librarians hired for these two positions, and the duties they are expected to perform.[6,7] In the case of the collection development librarian, these qualities include such general characteristics as "broad education and knowledge" and "ability to get along with many types of people,"[8] as well as specific duties such as expertise in materials budget allocation, the application of knowledge of the publishing world to materials selection, appropriate use of political and organizational skills to work effectively with faculty, selectors, and acquisitions personnel in developing the collections, and, probably most important, the ability to communicate effectively at all levels and in all situations.

Some of these skills, qualities, and duties are of the utmost importance, but they are not necessarily nor ordinarily specifically addressed in the evaluation document. Collection development librarians who make no effort to learn about the climate of the institution for which they work, and thus do not anticipate new developments, such as a new academic program, a new community group needing information, or an emerging field, will continually fail or at least fall short of basic expectations. If these expectations are not addressed specifically in the evaluation process, the deficiencies could go undetected for years, and when discovered, might be of such dramatic proportion that they would certainly be more difficult to resolve promptly or without rancor.

Qualities for the acquisitions librarian tend to be characterized in terms of actual duties, such as ability to order and receive materials efficiently and effectively, vendor selection, vendor performance evaluation, accounting expertise, appropriate application of knowledge of approval plans, supervisory ability, and receipt and disposition of gifts and exchange materials.[9] How often are these tasks and operations included in evaluation documents? Supervision is possibly the only one that is customarily addressed, and the evaluation of supervisory skills tends to be subjective.

The acquisitions librarian has the weighty responsibility of selecting the most appropriate source for the material to be ordered, in some cases finding the best price, ordering, receiving and processing the material before cataloging, possibly completing the accounting paperwork, and accomplishing all of this before the requestor asks about the status of the order. Attention to detail, swift follow-up, astute business practices, negotiation, superb organizational and communication skills are essential for effective acquisitions work. Do we address these responsibilities in our evaluations? While they do lend themselves to some clear methods of quantitative and qualitative evaluations, I suspect not.

INCREASING SCOPE OF RESPONSIBILITY

The traditional qualities, duties, and responsibilities of collection development and acquisitions librarians have expanded in scope as the field of librarianship has become more complex over the years.[10] The duties of collection development librarians have increased, requiring the librarians to be thoroughly knowledgeable about the institution's research, teaching, mission, trends, new programs, and goals. In addition to an intimate and broad knowledge of their institution, the librarians must be well-informed on the constantly changing climate in publishing, economics of the book trade, trends and new products in library automation, and thorough understanding of collection analysis methods and interpretation of data.

Similarly, acquisitions functions have increased in scope and difficulty. The acquisitions librarian must be able to not only order and receive materials for the library, but be familiar also with the impact and the challenge of automation in acquisitions functions.[11] Electronic means of acquiring materials have required the acquisitions librarian to be an expert in on-line acquisitions including compatibility with vendor systems and products. Responsibility for materials fund accounting through the use of on-line systems has brought with it opportunities to create instant reports on the use of funds, the performance of vendors, the speed of acquisition, and so on. In some cases, the use of on-line acquisitions systems have resulted in an increase of staff to enter bibliographic records for materials as or before they are even selected. Both acquisitions and collection development librarians are expected to be intimately acquainted with the details of serials pricing and the issues involved in spiraling periodical costs. New areas of expertise appear with regularity, and with them comes the expectation that the collection development and acquisitions librarians will become experts in the latest development or trend.

CONCLUSION

Some librarians may be uncomfortable with a rigorous performance evaluation system. They may fear that it will infringe on their professional freedom. Each library must decide on an evaluation system appropriate to its climate and needs, but it seems that one emphasizing the importance of the librarians' responsibilities might be to everyone's advantage, especially if presented and understood in a positive manner.

Collection development and acquisitions librarians and their supervisors cannot ignore the importance of planning the evaluation process, and gearing evaluations to specific duties and responsibilities. Although the tendency has been to make evaluations general, this is quite possibly against our best interest in libraries. Librarians would benefit from clearly defined expectations, and supervisors would likely benefit from increased communication that will result in enhanced job performance and more positive interaction.

Librarians are a substantial investment, especially those who have responsibility for the acquisition and development of the collections, and libraries should be prepared to devote extra attention to ensuring that the librarians are performing well. This cannot be done without a responsible and carefully planned personnel evaluation system, one which is fair and is related directly to the librarian's position. Preparation for the process is critical for it will result in the evaluations being less onerous, and it has an added benefit: it will assure others in the library and outside that the collection development and acquisitions librarians are carrying out their responsibilities in an exemplary, knowledgeable, and professional manner.

122   *Evaluating Acquisitions and Collection Management*

REFERENCES

1. Person, Roland. Library Faculty Evaluation: An Idea Whose Time Continues To Come. *Journal of Academic Librarianship* 5:142-147, July 1979.
2. Kroll, H. Rebecca. Beyond Evaluation: Performance Appraisal as a Planning and Motivational Tool in Libraries. *Journal of Academic Librarianship* 9:27-32, March 1983.
3. Dragon, Andrea C. Measuring Professional Performance: A Critical Examination. In: *Advances in Library Administration and Management, Volume 3*. Greenwich, CT, JAI Press Inc., pp. 24-46, 1984.
4. Reneker, Maxine and Virginia Steel. Performance Appraisal: Purpose and Techniques. In: *Personal Administration in Libraries*, 2nd edition, ed. by Sheila Creth and Frederick Duda. New York, Neal-Schuman Publishers, Inc., pp. 152-220, 1989.
5. Kennedy, Gail A. The Relationship Between Acquisitions and Collection Development. *Library Acquisitions: Practice and Theory* 7:225-232, 1983.
6. Futas, Elizabeth. Wanted: Collection Development Officer. *Collection Building* 4:55-56, 1982.
7. Bryant, Bonita. Allocation of Human Resources for Collection Development. *Library Resources & Technical Services* 30:149-162, January/March 1986.
8. Ryland, John. Collection Development and Selection: Who Should Do It? *Library Acquisitions: Practice and Theory* 6:13-17, 1982.
9. Myrick, William J. The Education of Mr. X. *Library Acquisitions: Practice and Theory* 2:195-198, 1978.
10. Johnson, Peggy. Collection Development Officer, a Reality Check: A Personal View. *Library Resources & Technical Services* 33:153-160, April 1989.
11. Henn, Barbara J. Acquisitions Management: The Infringing Roles of Acquisitions Librarians and Subject Specialists—An Historical Perspective. In: *Advances in Library Administration and Organization, Volume 8*. Greenwich, CT, JAI Press, Inc., pp. 113-129, 1989.

On Performance Consultation
with Bibliographers:
A Non-Rational
and Non-Machiavellian Perspective

Anthony M. Angiletta

SUMMARY. This article addresses the phenomenon of performance evaluation and performance appraisal as it applies to collection development librarians and the manner in which such specific evaluation is placed within a general organizational mode of performance appraisal. The position is taken that "performance appraisal" is tied to the rational-bureaucratic model of organizational behavior and is subject to corruption, personalism, and various manifestations of machiavellianism — all of which the model is expected to limit or eliminate. While "performance appraisal" is required for organizational control, the author suggests it be understood with and in the context of "performance consultation." The article also outlines basic performance criteria for collection development librarians.

INTRODUCTION

The question of performance evaluation or performance appraisal of those professional librarians who travel under an assortment of names — bibliographers, selectors, reference bibliographers, curators, collection development and management specialists — is subject to the same tension found in the nature and function of performance evaluation for all professional librarian positions and for most paraprofessional positions as well. That tension is perhaps evi-

Anthony M. Angiletta is Curator of the Social Sciences, Chief of Reference, and Acting Chief of Foreign Language and Area Collections, 6004 Green Library, Stanford University Libraries, Stanford, CA 94305.

dent immediately to the reader who discerns that a particular frame of reference is already implicit by the very use of the terms "performance evaluation" and "performance appraisal."

Both terms receive their primary meaning from a human context which assumes that a set of rational-bureaucratic and organizational control attitudes, behaviors and procedures are requirements for academic libraries to be successful utility maximizers. This is accompanied as well by the assumption that the more structurally differentiated and the more functionally specialized libraries are—ARL libraries with 100 or more staff members, as an arbitrary index of the type of research library we mean—the more there is a need for rational-bureaucratic, organizational-control mechanisms. To some extent as well, the fact that professional librarianship, while being one of the "helping professions," is a domain where the classical "autonomous professional" model is decidedly subordinate to the dominant model of the "organizational professional," also provides context for the terms "evaluation" and "appraisal."

The tension met in human settings where one assumes the right and need to assess the behavior of others for reasons of institutional effectiveness and efficiency has, on the one hand, to do with levels of generalization and levels of specificity, and, on the other hand, to do with age-old issues of human corruption—that is, of the seven deadly sins variety found in the *saligia* as well as the spectrum of mere venalities that organizational cultures create, sustain and promote.

Putting aside morality and amorality, libraries as bureaucratic organizations most often seek for purposes of control, efficiency, and equity to achieve universality rather than particularism in the establishment of norms of conduct and performance criteria as well as uniformity and consistency rather than diversity and inconsistency in their application. While this may vary across the professional-paraprofessional divide, the saw "different strokes for different folks," at least rhetorically and formally, is not a commonly encountered approach to norm creation and norm application.

This value placed on universality and uniformity can lead to enormous investments and reinvestments of organizational time devoted to establishing criteria for performance which exist across structure and function, which are rigorously tied only to behavior and never to attitude, and which still leave room for differentiating one function from another, one job description from another, one situation from another, and one person from one another in the manifold of time. While there are differences between public and private institutions, and differences across the professional-paraprofessional divide, annual salary-setting processes and events also influence and are influenced by performance appraisal processes. (And, to the extent that salary setting processes are also subject to universality and uniformity, we may expect to see attempts — noble and imaginative in some cases, preposterous in others — to achieve language and numerical ranking equivalencies.)

If performance appraisal processes in the rational-bureaucratic and organizational control model do not succeed in being rational, if they do not succeed in protecting against personalistic control, if they are structured in such a way as to produce an outcome or grade based on universal and uniform language at some distance from actual people and actual job experiences, thereby producing dehumanizing rather than merely impersonal interactions, one should seriously question whether the model is the appropriate one, or whether, as is frequently done, it is given lip service for both good and bad. Most often, the rational-bureaucratic model is corrupted when it is reified or taken to be "real," or when librarians spend large numbers of hours seeking to refine the language and putative behaviors taken as needed to make it "real." The actual value of the rational-bureaucratic model is heuristic and rhetorical; that is, it is at best, a guide to behavior, not a blueprint or a prescription. Finally, the terms "performance appraisal" and "performance evaluation" are almost invariably tied to the ideal-typic rational-bureaucratic mind set, and, hence, rather than being terms associated with relationships over time between mentors and colleagues, they become bureaucratic, time-bound, events of overseeing, providing ample opportunity for the intrusion of those abusive and manipulative behaviors that they, in principle, are to help prevent.

While organizational control may require that some documentation be kept concerning levels of performance for the good of the organization and for the good of the staff member, the position favored here is one which focuses not on a given event, which gives rise to given documents employing universal and uniform language, but on a continuous horizontal relationship between professional colleagues which, while punctuated by time-bound control documentation directed at grades and accountability—a kind of necessary quick dose of vertical power relations—might be best termed "performance consultation" rather than "performance evaluation" or "performance appraisal." What is implied by "performance consultation" is the idea of dialogue in a series of meetings over time, not necessarily tied to or driven by a salary setting or promotion cycle, which are *ad hoc* and scheduled, and exist for the purposes of conversing about what the other person is doing, where they are going, where they've been, what problems they have encountered, how they might be mediated or remedied, what the fit is between what the person is doing, what the job is, and what the organizational needs are. It is not, in the first instance, directed at documenting lists of goals and objectives, either for future or past accountability, autocritiques, and the production of grades. Nor is it a perspective which allows for statistically valid and reliable comparisons across functions and job descriptions or precise language equivalencies (both of which represent the highest ideal of management theory at least since 1883 when Sir Francis Galton published the first "scientific" merit rating scale). Indeed, much as with the proper relationship between professor and graduate student, the grade will take care of itself; what really counts is the type and duration of contact for the purposes of mentoring, facilitation, reminders where needed of the expectations of each in their social contract, and mutual learning and sharing of information. Such an approach as this is time-consuming and labor-intensive, but, if, in fact, you want to actually know your colleagues and their work, and actually be a participant in and partially responsible for their success, then moving beyond incidental contact and telescoped performance events is the only way that a responsible person charged with coordinating rather than commanding can succeed.

PERFORMANCE CONSULTATION WITH SELECTORS

One of the critical reasons that the perspective in favor here is one not solely based on a calendar-year or performance-period perspective, rests in the fact that the various elements of what selectors engage in occur unevenly and at different rates and are only partially controllable by the selector herself. In the performance appraisal event perspective, besides the scientism which cloaks human frailties in both the overseer and person being overseen, there is always the danger, again, of reification and, also, to borrow from constitutional argument, of strict constructionism; that is, with regard to reification, there can be a tendency in reviewing how well goals and objectives have been accomplished or in construing the next year's menu to take that list as the person and as that person's worth (at least, for that review period). With regard to "strict constructionism," the periodic performance event can transform what should be a mutually beneficial and constructive interaction into a social bargaining or negotiating session. When this intervenes, either or both the manager and the employee may seek to restrict the conditions of the discussion and evaluation to precisely what was agreed to last year. Again, the focus may be on the balance sheet rather than on the person.

What then does one look for in terms of providing a context for continuing performance consultation between whomever is charged with oversight and the individual selector as well as providing for the sake of those punctuated bureaucratic moments when a performance event must take place. Is there a list of performance categories which provide the backdrop for conversation, constructive criticism, and, if necessary, the basis for salary recommendations? A quote from an internal memorandum drafted by the author to selectors indicates the flavor of the process as well as the categories providing the basis for discussion:

> In seeking a common vocabulary with shared meanings for curatorial and bibliographer self-appraisal, our one-on-one conferences together, and the appraisal documents that emerge in the annual process, and also for understanding each other's expectations over the longer term, the attached list of curatorial and bibliographer task areas is put forth as a suggested guideline to thought, dialogue and action. Some or all of it painfully belabors the obvious or is that which we take for granted. But a revisit never hurts and can prevent misunderstanding. Also, the list as a whole is not canonic in its exhaustiveness. Nor are its categories necessarily mutually exclusive. However, they do provide a foundation for our discussions.

The basic list of performance categories for selectors that is favored here has six areas of activities. While the first two areas are usually weighted more than the others, there is always kept in mind where and how selectors operate, under what constraints and in what operational milieus they operate (branch selectors in multifunctional settings vs. reference bibliographers vs. "pure" collection developers, etc.), and what are the actual number and kinds of selection assignments they have.

A. *Collection Development and Management Activities*
1. Routine selection and accession activities directed toward the general collections.
2. Non-routine selection and accession activities (e.g., initiatives taken for on-going or concluded accessions of special collections and their processing and disposition).
3. Collection evaluation work.
4. Collection review work.
5. Collection preservation and conservation.
6. Budget management.
7. Staff supervision.
8. Consortial work as applied to 1, 3, 4, 5.
B. *Faculty/Staff/Programmatic Liaison.* What is the nature and extent of relationships with relevant faculty, departments, centers, and students? What courses did you give? Special forms of assistance? How well do you keep up with your disciplines?
C. *Intradepartmental Relations.* What is the character of your relations with departmental or unit colleagues?
D. *Interdepartmental and Interlibrary Relations.* What is the character of your relations with other local units and libraries?
E. *Professional Contributions.* What scholar librarian activities are you engaged in? Research-in-progress? Publications? Non-titular office holding in learned societies or associations, conference organizing, papers or lectures given, etc.?

Again, while local operational context is conditioning and, while "A" and "B" constitute the core of one's expectations (and where appropriate, donor relations and fundraising activities as found in "E"), this list indicates the range of activities that selectors engage or might engage in. There are, of course, other factors which come into play, including such things as context, "the whole," and contingency and fate. As one might imagine as well from the perspective adopted here, this is not a checklist with percentage proportions which is produced for each "performance event" and into which, in ledger-like fashion, values are entered, one after the other, in order to arrive at a quantity called a "grade." Rather, the approach is as much a "gestalt" or "integrated whole" approach as any other, focusing not on any particular element or giving equal attention to each (thus providing ample opportunity for "leveraged" conversations and both machiavellianism and ingratiation), but on the "forest" that the near-time and whole-past career represent as well as the way that life-course continues to be congruent with that of the organization.

The point has already been clearly implied that the rational-bureaucratic model has never succeeded in eliminating arbitrariness, capriciousness, and unreasonableness. It has also been at least implied that the model as actually enacted in the "lived lives" of organizations such as libraries provides the social psychological setting for a variety of behaviors, both noble and perverse, both systemic and individual, which are worthy of observation in a detached way. Most of us, however, are either participants or, at best, participant-observers. In an organizational or corporate setting, we are all reviewed for our performances. Some of us are gamesmen and manipulators. Some of us are ingratiators. Most of us actually try to take people at face value, recognize the achievements as well as inherent weaknesses of bureaucratic approaches, and focus on making judgments about people which are empirically and ethically informed, but rarely, if ever, conclusive and true. For the moment we think us so capable, back we go to certain moral failings such as pride and the sure knowledge of sloth in others.

REFERENCES

The literature on performance appraisal and performance evaluation is immense and occupies an important place in the literature of so-called management science. See, *inter alia,*

Poel, J.H.R. van de. *Judgment and Control*. Groningen: Wolters-Noordhoff, 1986.

Performance Evaluation: A Management Basic for Librarians. Phoenix: Oryx Press, 1986.

Douglas McGregor, "An Uneasy Look at Performance Appraisal," *Harvard Business Review*, September, 1972, p. 133 *ff*

N.B. Winstanley, "Legal and Ethical Issues in Performance Appraisals," *Harvard Business Review*, November-December, 1980, p. 186 *ff*.

The literature on Machiavellianism and various other forms of behavior in organizations is also extensive, both in the areas of management science and organizational studies, and in the psychological and behavioral sciences areas. Some examples include, *inter alia*,

Christie, R. and Geis, F. *Studies in Machiavellianism*. New York: Academic Press, 1970.

Hollon, C.J. "Machiavellianism and managerial work attitudes and perceptions." *Psychological Reports* 52:423-424, 1983.

Hughes, C.L. *Goal Setting*. New York: *American Management Association*, 1965.

Jones, Edward Ellsworth. *Ingratiation: A Social Psychological Analysis*. New York: Appleton-Century-Croft, 1964.

Leal, Alma Gloria. *An Investigation of Machiavellianism and Locus of Control in Selected Chicano and Anglo Administrators*. 1980.

Lefcourt, Herbert M. *Locus of Control*. Hillsdale: Erlbaum, 1982.

Kets de Vries, M.F.R. and Miller, D. *The Neurotic Organization*. San Francisco: Jossey-Bass, 1984.

La Bier, D. "Bureaucracy and psychopathology." *Political Psychology* 2(4):223-243, 1983.

Lerner, Allan W. *The Manipulators*. Hillsdale: Erlbaum, 1990.

_____. "Ambiguity and organizational analysis." *Administration and Society* 17(4):461-480, 1986.

Maccoby, M. *The Gamesman*. New York: Bantam Books, 1978.

March, J. and Olsen, J. *Ambiguity and Choice in Organizations*. Bergen: Universitetsforlaget, 1979.

Schein, Edgar H. *Organizational Culture and Leadership*. San Francisco: Jossey-Bass, 1985.

Siegel, J.P. "Machiavellianism, MBAs, and managers," *Academy of Management Journal* 16(3):404-411, 1973.

Solar, D. and Bruehl, D. "Machiavellianism and locus of control," *Psychology Reports* 29:1079-1082, 1979.

EVALUATING SPECIFIC ACQUISITIONS PROCESSES

Evaluation of Searching

Mae M. Clark

SUMMARY. Bibliographic searching entails verification and searching. Which of these functions is considered primary depends on many local factors and varies with the perspective of the different departments which rely on the searching. Development of an effective and smoothly operating searching unit requires evaluation. Evaluation refers to identifying goals, translating these goals into measurable indicators of goal achievement, collecting data about these factors and finally comparing the data gathered with the goal criteria. The two basic methods in which searching can be evaluated, statistical compilation and analysis of procedures, are discussed. Methods of statistical evaluation such as counting, determination of unit costs, monitoring tasks and staff time, sampling, etc., as well as work flow analysis, are discussed. While no one method will give a complete representation of how well the searching unit functions, by using a combination of the evaluation tools outlined and some subjective evaluation obtained through discussions with other departments, it is possible to evaluate searching, then identify and correct problems. Problems that can interfere with achieving the goals of the searching unit are discussed and methods for dealing with the problems are suggested.

Mae M. Clark is Associate University Librarian, Acquisitions Department, University of Florida Libraries, Gainesville, FL 32611.

131

INTRODUCTION

Bibliographic searching has been defined as containing two elements: searching and verification.[1] Verification refers to the bibliographic and price data. Bibliographic data includes the correct form of the author's name, the title, publisher, publishing date, the cost and the availability of the item. Many requests received in the searching unit are either incomplete or incorrect. Often requests are received in the searching unit for items that are unavailable because they are not yet published or for items that are out-of-print and are therefore unavailable through regular channels. The verification procedure identifies these items. Searching concerns the local library's situation. Does the library already own the item, are multiple copies needed, has the item been ordered but not received. Is the item part of a series received on standing order?

ROLE OF SEARCHING

Where this searching and verification is done varies from place to place within libraries depending on the size and type of the library. Public libraries or schools operating as part of a larger system may use selection lists which have already been presearched by the central processing center. In small libraries where specialization is less likely, public service personnel may perform the searching duties before sending the request to a clerk for order production. Within research libraries which have complex organizational structures, the searching unit has usually been located in one of several different areas: collection development, technical services or in a separate department of its own. There is no one "right" place for the searching unit. Often the location of the searching unit within an organization is based on personalities and skills of the staff. A very important skill in a searching unit is knowledge of foreign languages. Because a Cataloging Department often has personnel with this ability, searching units are occasionally composed of members from Cataloging because this skill is needed in both areas. Sometimes searching must share equipment such as computer terminals or copy machines with other departments so the two units are located near each other. Bibliographic or pricing tools such as *Books in Print* which must be shared can also be another reason for locating the searching unit in close proximity to another department. Regardless of the physical location of the searching unit, what must be realized is that whichever of these elements is considered the primary function of the unit will vary according to the perspective of different departments in the organization who must rely on searching.

To Collection Development searching may be the most important function, rather than verification. Once it is determined that the library does not own the item, collection development librarians may believe the request is ready for ordering. The importance of verifying that the item is actually available may not be so apparent to collection development librarians, especially when they are holding a glossy advertisement for it. They have identified a need for the item and want it ordered and received as quickly as possible. Cataloging may want the searching unit to emphasize the accuracy and completeness of the bibliographic record so that processing the item can be expedited upon its receipt. Careful searching of the library's holdings to avoid duplication of items in a series is also important to the Cataloging Department. However, cost verification is of no importance to cataloging. If the searching unit is a part of the Acquisitions Department, the emphasis could be placed on spending the materials budget. In that case, little searching could be done and items could be ordered with vendors being sent lists of ISBN's. This could spend the materials budget quickly but would lengthen the time required for cataloging. If requests were sent directly to suppliers with no searching done, the inaccurate information supplied, duplicate requests, and unavailable material ordered would cause the cost per item received to be unacceptably high. Relations with suppliers would most likely deteriorate as well. Since work done by the searching unit is also viewed by the book wholesaler or jobber in the form of orders the quality of preorder searching can affect the supplier's impression of how well the acquisitions department and the library as a whole are functioning. If the rate of duplicates or the number of items being returned as ordered incorrectly rises sharply, the supplier notices the fact quickly.

For a searching unit to be truly effective, however, both searching and verification are essential and must be balanced. The unit must search an item adequately to avoid duplication but at the same time sufficient requests must be searched to spend the materials budget. It does no good for each order request to be searched so thoroughly that few items are sent on for order production. It is difficult enough to balance the constant demand to produce high quality, accurate, completely searched requests at a certain speed but searching is made more difficult by the fact that there are outside conditions which affect the unit's work. One such condition is that the searching unit is completely dependant for its work on people who are often in another department and who therefore have other assigned duties which often take priority over filling out order requests. Requests are submitted by faculty members or bibliographers and selectors in fluctuating quantities, with differing levels of accuracy and completeness of information, and at intermittent times throughout the year. As the fiscal year draws to a close, fund managers often realize monies are not completely committed and the searching unit is deluged with requests. The large variations in the number of requests to be searched make it difficult to plan for staffing. Even though other departments, such as cataloging, are also dependent on others for their work, it is the responsibility for processing enough orders to spend the materials budget that creates additional pressure on the searching unit. With these various demands being made on the searching unit, it is necessary that an understanding of each department's processes and problems be held by all concerned. Otherwise, wasted effort, slow response time and high unit costs are the result.

PRELIMINARY STEPS TO EVALUATION

In order to assess how well the searching unit is responding to all of these demands, some methods of evaluation must be in place. Evaluation as used in this paper refers to identifying goals, translating these goals into measurable indicators of goal achievement, collecting data about these indicators and finally comparing the data gathered with the goal criteria.[2] Much of the evaluative work done in technical services has emphasized gathering statistics about what the department or unit is doing and has overlooked analyzing the quality of the work performed. Statistics can be found for the number of volumes added, number of periodical subscriptions held, percent increase or decrease of the materials fund, etc. While these are necessary and useful statistics to have, they do not address the issue of how well the library and in particular the searching unit is meeting its goals.

The first step to successful evaluation is to state the goals and objectives to be evaluated in clear, specific, and measurable terms. The goals are what the searching unit hopes to accomplish over a specific period of time. Such goals could include searching 15,000 order cards within six months, or encumbering a certain percentage of the materials budget every three months. If the goals are clearly stated, there can be no misunderstanding between staff and management about what is to be attempted. The goals must be specific so that they can be translated into operational terms. State the number of cards to be searched or the dollar amount to be encumbered so that it can be measured. To simply state that the goal is to search all order requests is too vague. Finally, identify methods to measure whether or not the goal was reached and if the goal was not reached, what prevented reaching the goal.[3]

By monitoring the demand placed on the searching unit and the unit's response to the demand, management predictions can be made. Information can be gained about the workload distribution among staff. Any special training or necessary skills, such as languages, can be identified. The establishment of realistic staff productivity goals and some measurement of acceptable levels of staff performance can be set. Information gathered helps to identify procedures which cause duplication of effort, wasted time and, therefore, money. Through evaluating the workflow, necessary changes in procedures can be identified and the efficiency of the unit can be increased. Changes in automation, new programs being offered and increases or decreases in the materials budget all affect procedures and work in the searching unit. By tracking fluctuations over a period of time, patterns may be revealed which should be considered in managing the unit. One word of caution must be offered, however. Evaluation procedures must be carefully designed so that the correct amount of information is gathered. Staff could spend so much time gathering information about how they work or counting order requests that actual production suffers. All items timed or counted must result in useful information.[4]

METHODS OF EVALUATION

There are two basic methods in which searching can be evaluated; either through statistical compilation or by an analysis of procedures. Statistical compilation can take many forms. It can be as straight forward as counting various kinds of incoming order requests, such as RUSH orders or orders for course reserves, foreign orders and out-of-print requests. Searching may be asked to count order cards submitted by subject area or special fund number. However, not all requests received result in an order being placed so it is important to monitor the number of other types of requests received as well. To get a more complete picture of demands being made on the searching unit, requests for items that are already in the collection, items which will come on approval, or out-of-print requests from dealers' catalogs that are outdated must be counted as well. All of this information helps complete the picture of work being done by the searching unit. By identifying areas that require special handling or orders that require a staff member with special skills, the searching unit head will be able to assign staff more effectively. An analysis of the unit's workflow may identify areas that need additional staff, or areas where duplication of effort is taking place. Duplication of steps in the searching and verification procedures not only increases unit costs but it lengthens the amount of time required before the item can reach the patron. Therefore, an analysis of workflow in the searching unit should be done on a regular basis and especially if changes in automation are taking place.

In addition to this basic counting, other statistics concerning searching can be gathered. Unit costs within a particular library can be measured. This can be done in several different ways. Lancaster discusses several methods of determining unit costs in *The Measurement and Evaluation of Library Services*.[5] One means of arriving at the unit cost of an item is simply to add the salary costs of all those involved in processing an order from the time it is received in the searching unit until it is received, paid for, and sent to cataloging and divide this amount by the number of items received. To get the unit cost for searching, one would add all of the salaries of the searching unit and divide it by the number of items searched. For instance, if total personnel costs for the unit were $125,000 and the unit searched 27,000 order cards, the unit cost would be 125/27 or about $4.63 per request.

Tuttle[6] discusses another method for presenting technical processing costs by relating the costs of technical processing to the costs of the library materials purchased. She calls this the TSCOR. The TSCOR can be obtained by dividing the total salary expenditure for technical processing procedures during a specified period by the total amount spent on purchased materials during the same time. The TSCOR then indicates the costs of technical processing for each dollar spent on the purchase of materials. For example, if a library spends $1,750,000 a year to purchase materials and the personnel costs are $850,000, the TSCOR would be $850/1,750 or $0.48. That is, the library spends $0.48 in technical processing salaries for every dollar it spends to purchase materials. To arrive at a TSCOR for the searching unit, one would add all of the salaries of the searching unit and divide it by the total dollar amount of the items searched.

Another method of statistics gathering requires timing each task to determine how long it takes for an order request to be processed from the time it is received in searching until the request is forwarded to the order unit. This method requires searchers to identify each step in the searching procedure and monitor the amount of time spent doing each one. When this is divided by the number of items searched, an average amount of time for each step is realized. Searching times can be gathered for the amount of time used in searching the main catalog or local database, as well as the time required for searching the national bibliographic utility and the amount of time needed to verify the price. These times can be particularly useful in estimating the number of searching staff needed when the number of special orders such as RUSH items or out-of-print requests increases. Workflow adjustments can be made if searching staff must share computer terminals or price verification tools with other departments. Terminals and verification tools can then be scheduled based on very specific data.

Yet another way of evaluating searching is to have searchers fill out time logs and then count the number of orders searched in a given amount of time. One can get an idea of the number of orders that can be searched in a week or month and thereby plan for staffing. Often personnel are surprised at the many interruptions in a day that reduce time spent on searching. In a study done at the University of North Carolina at Chapel Hill, a combination of these procedures was used. The searchers completed time logs identifying the type of material being searched and also recorded the number of hours worked per day. This gave management a more precise record of the work performed in the selection and identified interruptions which reduced the amount of time available for searching.[7] Committee work, training new employees, writing manuals and planning library moves in addition to vacations and holidays, coffee breaks and the occasional illness can all interrupt a searcher's concentration and interfere with the unit's work. If time logs identifying these potential interruptions are not maintained, management may be under the erroneous impression that staff are devoted to searching eight hours per day and may not understand why more order requests are not being searched. While it is true that time available to searching will vary from week to week, if the time logs are kept for long periods of time, patterns will become visible. For instance, in an academic library, time devoted to searching may decrease in the fall if part-time workers must be hired and trained every year. This loss may be offset within a few months when all of these workers are fully trained. If supervisors are aware of this pattern, a decrease in requests searched will be expected in the fall with the understanding that searching will increase in a few months. However, if something should interfere with this pattern, such as library construction or departmental reorganization, management should be aware that additional staff will be required if the same number of orders are to be searched as in previous years.

Sampling provides yet another means of gathering statistics about the tasks being performed by the searching unit. Instead of counting all order requests or monitoring how staff time is spent on an on-going basis, sampling techniques allow management to make generalizations by examining only a small fraction of the population. In reality, it is a shortcut that extends the librarian's range of data-gathering activities. In *Scientific Management of Library Operations* Dougherty and Heinritz discuss the differences between attribute and variable sampling and then consider the three major aspects of the sampling process: deciding on sample reliability; determining the sample size required to achieve this reliability; and selecting the sample.[8] Since sampling studies only a small number of the possibilities, the results are not as reliable as the results would be if each variable were counted individually. The librarian must decide before beginning how certain the results must be. The more certainty the librarian demands, the larger the sample size will have to be. If done correctly, sampling can be used to determine the same types of information which were gathered through counting each item but the information can be gathered in less time. Information collected could include data about the percentage of order requests that are for RUSH or out of print items, or the percentage of the searching unit's time that is actually spent searching, or the percentage of order requests that are for items published abroad or any other item of information which might be helpful.

One final method of evaluating a searching unit is through workflow analysis. An analysis of workflow procedures is helpful when evaluating searching so that any procedures not operating smoothly can be adjusted. One way of doing this is to make a flowchart indicating the path an order request takes. During times of high staff turnover or when a library is changing from a manual to an automated system, these workflow charts can become the basis for training programs or manuals.[9] However, it is important to consider the effect that changes in the procedures in one area will have on another. For example, if searching decides to select and download into the local on-line database any record from a national bibliographic utility rather than choose the LC authenticated record, the effect this decision could have on cataloging would be tremendous. Whereas previously, cataloging had received bibliographic information of a certain quality from the searching unit, now there is no agreed-upon standard. Unit cost for searching would be reduced because little evaluation of record selection would be done and the materials budget could be spent quickly, but cataloging processing time and, therefore, costs would increase.

DIFFICULTIES IN PERFORMING AN EVALUATION

While it is possible to evaluate searching through a number of different methods there are also difficulties associated with conducting the assessment. Even though it is relatively simple to gather statistical data, it is often impossible to apply the information gathered in one library to another. Variations may include the physical location of the searching unit, or the differences caused by searchers in one library using manual as opposed to an automated system. Interlibrary comparisons in such cases may be almost useless. For instance, if a research library ordering esoteric foreign material has determined that ten requests per hour is an acceptable number of requests for a searcher to complete, this quantity may be unacceptable to a public library ordering multiple copies of a best seller. Unit costs and TSCORs which are acceptable at one library may not be satisfactory at another library. A great deal of data can be gathered but because libraries can differ substantially from each other, the standards of one cannot always be applied to others.[10]

In addition to the issue of numerous differences that exist among libraries is the problem of methodology used to gather these statistics, especially the cost analysis data. In the past, the methodology used to obtain these figures was not specifically reported so it was impossible to replicate the data.[11] The literature did not include a detailed explanation of how and why the statistics were gathered in that manner so that other librarians who wished to compare their operations to the library in the report were unable to do so. Even though one may understand that interlibrary comparisons are not completely valid, it is often interesting and perhaps useful to compare statistics gathered at one's library with those collected at another. If the methodology is not carefully described, however, even this rough evaluation is not possible.

COMBINING METHODS OF EVALUATION

While no one method will give a complete representation of how well the searching unit is reacting to the various demands and responsibilities required of it, by using a combination of the measures outlined above, it is possible to evaluate searching. Using information from the statistics gathered through direct counting and by monitoring the unit cost, a supervisor can begin to assess the quality of the searching unit. If these figures are supplemented by data about the average length of time it takes to search an order, and by the amount of time spent by the staff on searching, the unit head can obtain a more complete representation of activities within the section.

After some months of statistics gathering, trends may become apparent. Perhaps during the year, times can be identified when the searching unit is overwhelmed with order requests and additional support should be assigned to the unit. Periods of time when searching is overstaffed could also be revealed. During those times, searching unit personnel might be temporarily reassigned to another unit in acquisitions or to cataloging. These two areas are the most obvious choices because the detailed knowledge required to understand bibliographic records is needed here. However, because searchers can interpret bibliographic records so easily, they could also assist the reference department if it were understaffed. A variety in responsibilities often provides a stimulus and helps to relieve the repetitive nature of searching. Searching unit personnel are often among the highest classification of paraprofessional help in the library. Searching order requests can become routine and boring unless specific attempts are made to circumvent such an atmosphere. Some combination of job assignments that utilizes the searcher's skills in other situations helps to avoid burnout which has been identified as a common problem in technical services personnel.[12] Other types of information about collection strengths and weaknesses may become apparent through data gathering. If it is discovered through this data collection that a high percentage of order requests are being received for items which are already in the collection or which will come on approval, discussions should be held with selectors to determine how they are making selection decisions. It is a waste of time for the selectors to fill out order requests for material that is already in the collection. It is frustrating to searchers who expect that most of the order requests will result in orders to search and then find that many of the items requested are already in the collection. If time logs indicate that a high proportion of the searching unit's time is being spent on training new employees, this would indicate a need for training manuals. If searchers are waiting for computer terminals that must be shared with other units, this would indicate a need for more computer terminals. While no one method of data collection will give a complete picture about the searching unit's work, by combining a number of these techniques an accurate assessment can be made.

SUBJECTIVE EVALUATION

After working with the searching unit for a period of time, a supervisor will also form a subjective measure of the unit's effectiveness which is another important method of evaluation. Since the searching, ordering and receiving units are interdependent on the quality of work each performs, inaccurate verification in the searching unit adversely affects the work of the other units. Wrong titles and duplicate copies being supplied by vendors create problems for receipts personnel and are often a direct reflection of the work produced in the searching unit. Wasted time and money in either returning the wrong titles or duplicates or in having to keep unwanted copies may be the result of inaccurate searching by the unit. Orders which must be claimed repeatedly from vendors also waste time and may be an indication of insufficient verification by searching staff.

Complaints from collection development about cards remaining in the searching unit for long periods of time are another subjective indication that there are problems which need attention. Problems such as these indicate that the searching unit needs either more personnel or personnel with additional skills for the amount and type of material being requested. For instance, it is possible that the searching unit is composed primarily of personnel recently hired and that recently received requests have been for microform sets, music scores, maps, or antiquarian German serials. These type of requests require an experienced searcher and are beyond the capability of newly trained staff. Careful monitoring of the types of requests received would reveal the cause of the searching backlog. The other possibility is that the unit is not performing adequately because of improperly spent time. Time logs which monitor how the searchers are spending their time and a flowchart of the searching procedures would identify possible duplicate steps in the workflow and aid in the resolution of this problem. The quality of record selection is another subjective indication of how well the searching unit is responding to its duties. If complaints on the quality of record selection are received from Cataloging, either communication between the departments is inadequate or the training of new searchers is not satisfactory. Maintaining close communication with these other library departments which rely on searching can assist the searching unit supervisor in evaluating the unit.

Unlike Cataloging, which may utilize the widely accepted MARC format, there are no universally agreed-upon standards defining an acceptably searched order request. Definitions will vary from library to library. Some decisions that need to be made at each library as they set standards for their institution concern price verification and whether or not the price of an item will affect the searching it receives. One library may want all of its orders to have the price verified regardless of the effort this entails but to another library price estimates may be acceptable. At some libraries, the price of an item may affect the amount of searching it receives. For instance, it an item is projected to cost $3.50 it may not be searched at all; it can simply be ordered with the understanding that if it is a duplicate only the $3.50 will have been wasted and not a great deal of staff time as well. Many times the least expensive items will consume the most time in a searching unit while verification of existence or availability is almost impossible. Another decision that needs to be made in defining standards for an institution might be the extent of searching necessary for titles published abroad. If searchers cannot identify them on national bibliographic utilities should letters requesting price and availability be sent or should orders be placed on the basis of a publisher's advertisement or catalog. Obviously, the twin goals of adequately searching an item so that the vendor can identify and supply it and searching enough orders to spend the budget must be reached if the unit is to be successful. Within each library decisions about the quality of searching required must be reached and the searching unit must be flexible enough to respond to changing demands. Some of the decisions concerning standards should be set within the unit but other decisions should be made in conjunction with collection development and cataloging.

Discussions with collection development staff should be held to determine areas for which searching will be responsible as well as those for which collection development will be responsible. Items to be discussed could cover a wide range of problems, such as the disposition of duplicates. A percentage of duplicates received which is acceptable might be negotiated. Even with the most careful searching and verification some duplicates will arrive. Must all of them be returned or can those that cost less than a certain amount be kept or forwarded to the gifts and exchange section? Another possible topic to discuss is the number of duplicate requests being received in searching. If there is a high percentage of requests for items already in the collection, this information should be communicated to collection development so that changes can be made in selection methods. Another type of duplicate order request is generated when multiple selectors use multiple copies of publishers catalogs thereby having several selectors choose the same title for the library. Perhaps some agreement about routing catalogs could be reached between collection development and searching. Some decisions about level of searching needed before order requests are completed and forwarded to the searching unit should be made. Should the requestor search the main catalog or on-line system before the requests are sent to searching or should no searching at all be done? Some method of assigning priorities and decisions about what is a reasonable amount of time to expect an order request to stay in the searching unit before it is either placed on order or returned to the bibliographer for additional information should be discussed. These are just a few examples of the concerns which should be discussed with collection development staff. These discussions can present an opportunity to exchange information about procedures and problems in both departments which will help each understand the functions of the other better.

Cataloging should be consulted so that agreement can be reached concerning the quality of the bibliographic record that should be chosen. Bibliographic records should be chosen which will help speed material to the user once it has been received and an invoice processed. However, because the priorities of the two units differ, the ideal record for cataloging may not be the one chosen. The bibliographic record which searching may choose for ordering purposes will not always be the one cataloging will use. In the case of large sets, for instance, it is more expedient to select the one series record for ordering purposes and let cataloging adjust the bibliographic records when the items are received. There should be a basic agreement with cataloging about standards of bibliographic records chosen by the searching unit. As changes in automation and other procedures occur, adjustments will need to be made in the decisions about which records should be selected. A continuing dialog between searching and cataloging is necessary just as it is with collection development.

CONCLUSION

The management of a bibliographic searching unit is a complicated administrative situation and to supervise it efficiently the librarian must evaluate personnel and procedures carefully. The librarian must acknowledge the needs of collection development and cataloging and yet be able to communicate the requirements of the searching unit to these departments. Negotiations between these departments and searching must be based on knowledge of the searching unit's performance. This knowledge can be gained through an evaluation made by using a combination of different techniques. Some of the techniques which can aid in making the evaluation are collecting statistics, determining unit costs, monitoring staff time, and forming subjective interpretations as demonstrated earlier in this paper. Basic information about number and types of order requests can be gathered through counting order cards. This helps to identify trends in order submission patterns, as well as to disclose the percentage of RUSH, RESERVE or other requests which require special handling or skills. In this manner the supervisor can predict changes which affect staffing needs. By having staff members complete time logs, the librarian can determine what interruptions are reducing time spent on searching. Unit costs can also be determined and compared at regular intervals to help in providing an evaluation.

In addition to these statistical items, subjective evaluation must also be made by the supervisor. Communication with collection development and cataloging, as well as ordering and receiving personnel in acquisitions, can assist in providing subjective information for the evaluation of searching. For example, ordering and receiving personnel will indicate whether or not verification is adequate. High rates of duplicates, orders for items that must be claimed several times, items ordered in error that must be returned are all indicators that the searching unit is not performing adequately. This might indicate that additional training is necessary. Searching backlogs will be observed and questioned by collection development. Additional personnel may be indicated if evidence suggests the unit is already working at capacity. Selection of poor quality records for ordering not only will delay items being cataloged, but will confuse vendors receiving the orders. Subjective data about the quality of the order record can be obtained through discussions between the unit head and the vendors at library association meetings or when vendors visit the library. With so many people interested in the outcome of searching, it is difficult to disguise an inadequate searching job but all too often a smoothly functioning unit goes unappreciated. Through careful evaluation of the unit's work, a supervisor will not only have necessary information to identify and explain problem areas which arise but will also have data to demonstrate how well the unit is working.

REFERENCES

1. G. Edward Evans, *Developing Library and Information Center Collections.* 2nd ed. Littleton, Co.: Libraries Unlimited, 1987, p. 215.

2. Charles A. Bunge, "Approaches to the Evaluation of Library Reference Services," in *Evaluation and Scientific Management of Libraries and Information Centers* by F.W. Lancaster and C.W. Cleverdon, Leyden: Noordhoff, 1977, p. 42.

3. *Ibid.*, p. 43.

4. American Library Association. RTSD/RS. Acquisitions Committee, "Statistics for Managing Acquisitions Operations," p. 3.

5. F.W. Lancaster, *The Management and Evaluation of Library Services*, Washington, DC: Information Resources, 1977, pp. 265-269.

6. H.W. Tuttle, "TSCORE: The Technical Services Cost Ratio," *Southeastern Librarian*. 1969, 19:15-25 in *Measurement and Evaluation of Library Services* by F.W. Lancaster. Washington, DC: Information Resources, 1977, pp. 265-266.

7. Janet L. Flowers, "Time Logs for Searchers: How Useful?" *Library Acquisitions: Practice and Theory.* 2(2):77-83, 1978.

8. Richard M. Dougherty and Fred J. Heinritz. *Scientific Management of Library Operations*. 2nd ed. Metuchen, N.J.: Scarecrow Press, 1982. pp. 211-233.

9. Rose Mary Magrill and John Corbin. *Acquisitions Management and Collection Development in Libraries*. 2nd ed. Chicago: American Library Association, 1989. pp. 251-252.

10. F.W. Lancaster. *The Measurement and Evaluation of Library Services*. Washington, DC: Information Resources, 1977, p. 266.

11. *Ibid.*, p. 265.

12. Shirley Leung, "Coping With Stress: A Technical Services Perspective," *Journal of Library Administration*. 5(1):11-19 (Spring 1984).

Service Through Automation:
Sharing Fund Accounting Information

Joyce L. Ogburn
Patricia Ohl Rice

SUMMARY. The Acquisitions Department of the Pennsylvania
State University Libraries performs centralized purchasing and
budgetary management for twenty campuses. Evaluation of Acquisitions' services revealed that existing paper-driven, partially on-line
accounting and reporting processes were unable to meet all constituent needs. Acquisitions recently implemented an on-line fund accounting system designed to enhance the processing and management information services that the department can offer to its
constituents. A Fund Accounting Implementation Team evaluated
the new system during design and implementation and continues to
monitor system and user performance in the post-implementation
phase.

INTRODUCTION

An acquisitions department functions primarily as a service unit
within the academic library, since its traditional tasks — obtaining
library materials, controlling expenditure of the materials budget,
and generating various management reports — are all performed for
the benefit of other organizational constituencies. Traditional client
groups served by acquisitions departments include collection development, library administration, library and/or university accounting, and university administration. Acquisitions' relationship with
these groups can be direct, as in the case of collection development,
library administration, and accounting, or indirect, as in the case of
university administration.

Joyce L. Ogburn is Order Librarian and Patricia Ohl Rice is Documentation
and Training Librarian at the Pennsylvania State University, E506 Pattee Library,
University Park, PA 16802.

149

Fund accounting is an essential component of acquisitions responsibilities. Collection development personnel are interested in
balances of specific amounts, funds, or fund groupings. Accounting
units, whether in the library or part of university-wide accounting
operations, are responsible for maintaining an institutional audit
trail. Library and university administrators have pressing needs for
management data to meet accountability requirements and to assist
in strategic planning.

Whenever one unit in an organization performs a service for
other organizational constituencies, it is natural for an element of
judgment or evaluation to enter the scene. Collection development
specialists want account balances on demand; accounting requires
paperwork to be both timely and accurate; administrators need management reports that simplify the planning process. In short, client
groups judge the effectiveness of the service-provider whenever
they experience a felt need. In addition, the service-provider performs continuous self-evaluation as it attempts to respond to clients'
expressed wishes. Such evaluation and self-evaluation can be either
formal or informal, although one suspects that in most academic
libraries the informal model prevails.

Pennsylvania State University Library (PSUL) has recently implemented a new Fund Accounting Control System (FACS) within
its LIAS database. After a brief description of LIAS, we will discuss the organization of acquisitions responsibilities at Penn State,
the needs of various groups for fund accounting information, and
the way in which the planning process accommodated the diverse
groups. We will detail some of the ways in which FACS meets user
needs and describe the mechanisms that have been put in place for
on-going evaluation of system and user performance.

LIBRARIES INFORMATION ACCESS SYSTEM (LIAS)

The backbone of PSUL automation efforts is the Libraries Information Access System (LIAS), which has been under continuous
development since the 1970s. LIAS has been designed with several
guiding philosophies in mind:

> These goals . . . include an independent operating environ-
> ment, a fully integrated system design, defined standards that

incorporate national and international standards, the ability to accommodate links with other systems and services, and mechanisms for resource sharing.[1]

The notion of integration has been particularly important to all of the constituent groups involved in the design of LIAS: each new component of the system is fully integrated with existing components, allowing users to switch readily among functions.[2] The diverse nature of Penn State's community has required a system that is as open as possible (within normal constraints of system security), available throughout the Commonwealth, easy for novices, and yet able to provide powerful retrieval capabilities for sophisticated users.[3]

In its present configuration, LIAS includes a bibliographic control system, which supports the creation and maintenance of bibliographic records in all formats; an on-line public access catalog; an inventory control function which manages the circulation of library materials at the main campus; a gateway to the Faxon SC-10 system (presently used for serials check-in); and the newly-released Fund Accounting Control System, which is a subsystem of the as yet undeveloped acquisitions system. In addition, LC MARC monograph tapes are routinely loaded into LIAS and are searchable by staff and patrons alike.

Future LIAS development plans include completion of the acquisitions system, on-line authority control, expansion of the inventory control system to other PSU campuses, and loading of additional LC MARC formats and other external tapes. Specifications for the acquisitions system call for six on-line functions: (1) initiation of order requests by library subject specialists; (2) pre-order searching; (3) order placement; (4) order monitoring and receiving; (5) fund accounting; and (6) capture and manipulation of management information.[4] The newly-developed fund accounting system brought the fifth and part of the sixth of these functions into realization.

CONSTITUENTS AND THEIR NEEDS

The constituents. The Acquisitions Department of Pennsylvania State University Libraries performs centralized purchasing and budgetary management for collection development specialists at the main campus and for nineteen branch campus librarians throughout the Commonwealth. In addition to ordering and receiving functions, Acquisitions is responsible for generating account status reports for collection development personnel at all locations and fund status reports to library administrators.

Acquisitions works closely with Library Accounting, which is administered by the Office of the Dean. Library Accounting expends the non-materials portion of the Libraries' budget: equipment, staff software, furniture, contractual services, professional travel, and the like. In addition, this office authorizes payments to library materials suppliers and reconciles library financial records with those of University Accounting Operations.

Collection development responsibilities are shared among Libraries faculty. The head librarians at the branch campus locations are designated as official collection development specialists for their locations. At the main campus, almost all librarians participate in collection development as subject specialists under the general direction of the Chief of Humanities and Social Sciences, the Chief of Science and Technology, and the Coordinator for Collection Development.

PSUL is considered an academic unit of Penn State, and hence is administered by a Dean of Libraries, assisted by three Assistant Deans and various support staff. The Dean of Libraries reports to the Executive Vice President and Provost of the University.

An important organizational contributor to library programs is Library Computing Services (LCS), administratively under the University's Computing and Information Services, but physically located within the main library. LCS is responsible for major library automation projects, including maintaining and developing the LIAS database, programming, telecommunications, hardware maintenance, and the like.

Constituent Needs. In recent years, the Acquisitions Department has been generally successful in meeting basic constituent needs: balances were provided on a monthly basis, and some annual management reports were generated. But ongoing informal evaluation by "client groups" and the department itself revealed the limitations of existing services. The outdated mainframe accounting system functioned in batch mode, allowed only one user at a time, was not available outside Acquisitions, and could not produce management reports. As a result, Acquisitions was forced to rekey data into microcomputer files for manipulation by programs such as Quattro in order to generate reports needed by collection development, administration, and Acquisitions management. The cost to Acquisitions in terms of staff time and energy was extremely high. Mainframe system limitations also forced on some constituents an account structure that did not adequately meet their collection development needs. A new fund accounting system, it was hoped, would allow Acquisitions to provide budgetary information on a more timely basis and in more sophisticated formats.

It was apparent from the outset that interested parties would differ in regard to the type and number of needs that they would want addressed by a new system. It was also recognized that the more general the need, the more likely it was to be shared by several constituents. Table 1 summarizes the kinds of needs which have to be met and how many of those needs were shared by the different constituents.[5]

Acquisitions, as the primary user of a new accounting system, clearly had the most complex requirements, ranging from general needs shared by all constituents (e.g., system security), to specific needs shared with only one other group (e.g., keyboarding economy). Closely aligned with Acquisitions were Library Accounting and Collection Development, two groups equally dependent on timely, accurate financial transactions and budget status information.

Library Computing Services shared general system needs with all users, but also had some specific requirements shared with few others (for example, system diagnostics). In addition, LCS shared with Library Accounting a need to develop a system that would eventually be capable of interfacing with the University's accounting system.

Library administration, as a direct "client" of the system, had a significant overlap in needs and expectations with other library groups. University administration, on the other hand, was interested in the system only insofar as it would assist the Dean to meet her responsibilities for accountability and strategic planning.

TABLE 1: FACS CONSTITUENT NEEDS RANKED BY TOTAL NUMBER SHARED

NEEDS	UNIV. ADMIN.	LIB. ADMIN.	LIB. COMPUTING SVCS.	COLL. DEVEL.	LIB. ACCTG	ACQUIS	TOTAL SHARED
1 System security	$	$	$	$	$	$	6
2 Data security	$	$	$	$	$	$	6
3 Differential access levels	$	$	$	$	$	$	6
4 Timely data	$	$	$	$	$	$	6
5 Quick response time		$	$	$	$	$	5
6 Meaningful system messages for users		$	$	$	$	$	5
7 Clear displays		$	$	$	$	$	5
8 Access by simultaneous users		$	$	$	$	$	5
9 Access at multiple locations		$	$	$	$	$	5
10 Report generator		$	$	$	$	$	5
11 24-hour availability		$	$	$	$	$	5
12 Immediate updating of the database		$	$	$	$	$	5
13 System prompts		$	$	$	$	$	5
14 Ease of use		$		$	$	$	4
15 Budget monitoring		$		$	$	$	4
16 Foreign currency conversion, updating, rates		$		$	$	$	4

	5	18	19	21	23	27	
17 Fund status in latest currency rates		$		$	$	$	4
18 Beginning & end of year transition support		$	$		$	$	4
19 Compatibility with University accounting system		$			$	$	3
20 Editing capability	$				$		2
21 Fiscal transaction					$	$	2
22 Review of session					$	$	2
23 Keyboarding economy					$	$	2
24 Notes field for special messages					$	$	2
25 Reconciliation of encumbrances & expenditures				$	$		2
26 Blocking & forcing use of funds				$	$		2
27 System journal reports			$		$		2
28 Transaction logs			$		$		2
29 Expenditures by selector-assigned categories					$		1
30 Shared access to data by special groups				$			1
31 System diagnostics for programmers			$				1
TOTAL NEEDS PER CONSTITUENT	5	18	19	21	23	27	

MEETING NEEDS THROUGH EVALUATION
AND PLANNING

In order to insure that as many needs as possible would be met by the new system, two planning groups were constituted. The first group was the LIAS Acquisitions Development Team, composed of representatives from Acquisitions, LCS, and two public service units of the Libraries. The development team concentrated on initial conceptual design of FACS. Once LCS began programming, another team took over guidance of the project.

In June of 1989, the LIAS Fund Accounting Implementation Team (FAIT) was appointed by the Acting Assistant Dean, Bibliographic Resources and Services Division. Chaired by the Chief of Acquisitions, the team included three key Acquisitions staff members (Order Librarian, Receipt Librarian, and Accounts Coordinator), the Libraries Accounting Supervisor, two representatives from the Libraries' Computer-Based Resources and Services Team (CBRST), two LCS staff members, and a documentation design specialist from technical services.[6]

The Fund Accounting Implementation Team was charged to guide and support the transition from concept to functioning system—the "birth" of FACS. As LCS programmed and mounted pre-release versions of FACS components, the team evaluated and provided feedback about record content, content designation, screen displays, report formats, search arguments, authorization levels, and the like. Immediately prior to release of FACS version 1.0, FAIT designed and ran an exhaustive system test. Once system stability was established, FAIT provided start-up training to Acquisitions and Accounting staff and tested the system under real operational conditions. Having completed system and operational evaluations, FAIT prepared documentation and offered training sessions for all other users. Acquisitions released FACS to the larger library community in March 1990.

FACS FEATURES

FACS supports constituent needs in two main ways: *directly* through access to the system and its data; and, perhaps more important, *indirectly* by allowing Acquisitions to have real time transactions, on-line currency conversion, expenditure management, and by enabling Acquisitions to perform complex and meaningful analyses.

Designed ultimately to function as a component of the future acquisitions system, FACS currently operates as a stand-alone subsystem within LIAS. In line with LIAS design philosophy, FACS

> maintains the "look and feel" of LIAS. Users familiar with LIAS and IPC [the inventory control function] will see many features that have been carried over from those systems, including ease and efficiency of use, record checking routines to minimize errors and consistent command usage.[7]

Authorized users can query fund accounting information from any LIAS terminal that supports staff processing activities. Switching between FACS and other LIAS components requires only a few keystrokes.

Several general features of FACS are worth mentioning at the outset. A major advantage of on-line, mainframe-based accounting is accessibility. FACS is available 24 hours a day except for Sunday mornings when LIAS is taken down for routine system maintenance. Since the Libraries, including the branch campuses, are "wired" to LIAS, FACS is available state-wide and can support multiple simultaneous users. Because FACS is fully interactive, transactions and edits performed in Acquisitions or Accounting instantly affect the system data and displays.

In an age of computer viruses, university administrations are deeply concerned about security, especially confidential budget information. FACS can be accessed only at staff terminals.[8] Data security is provided by journalization and daily back-ups. System security is protected by three levels of authorization: Acquisitions determines *who* can use the system, *what commands* each person can use, and *what data* a person can view, all determinations being based on the user's job responsibilities. For example, the Dean of Libraries needs to view all budgetary information in the system, but does not perform fiscal transactions; therefore, she is authorized to query all records, but not authorized to create, edit, encumber, liquidate, prepay, and so on. Collection development faculty are authorized to query only their own accounts. An Acquisitions assistant who orders monographs may perform all types of fiscal transactions, but only on monograph funds. Acquisitions librarians may query all data in the system, and several persons in Acquisitions are also authorized to create and edit FACS records. LCS staff are authorized to delete records and, of course, to maintain the necessary programming that drives the system. Various types of users may also be authorized to generate management reports from FACS data. Because of the careful approach to system and data security, the Libraries' need for confidentiality and protection against catastrophic loss or tampering has been met.

Several other general features of FACS derive specifically from the system "philosophy" of ease of use. The first item is an on-line Help for FACS commands, available to all users regardless of their level of authorization. The second feature is a series of system prompts that guide Acquisitions and Accounting personnel through fiscal transactions. Third is the concept of user default: to have keyboarding, the system itself supplies some or all of the search argument needed to query the records that a given user accesses most often. Another time-saver is a command repeat feature, which enables staff to perform a series of fiscal transactions on the same account without having to key in the entire transaction argument for the account.

Because FACS was designed specifically to track the allocation and expenditure of the Libraries' materials budget, record structure in FACS reflects a hierarchy of budgetary designations used by University and Libraries accounting operations. The lowest level of display is the Account Record, usually a subject designation, and the level at which fiscal transactions occur. At higher levels, the system summarizes fiscal activity by Type (e.g., monographs, new serials, binding, databases), Location (e.g., University Park, Altoona, Beaver), and by codes used by University administration to designate cost centers, funding sources, and procurement categories. Fiscal summaries at all levels provide allotment, encumbrance, expenditure and balance data.

Selectors desiring more specific subject tracking than can be provided by a broad subject account such as Education or Anthropology have the option of creating up to ninety-nine Categories within their Account Record. These Categories can represent any subject, format, language, or other breakdown the selector desires. For example, the Education selector could establish Categories for Bilingual Education, Mainstreaming, Introductory Textbooks, or any other designation that met the collection development needs of that particular area. Although Categories track only expenditures (items prepaid or paid for after receipt), many collection development faculty are looking forward to implementing Categories in their subject account.

The various levels of fiscal summary available in the system meet diverse user needs. Accounts and Categories clearly support collection development interests. Branch campus librarians, who are accountable equally to University Park Libraries administration and to their campus CEO's, need to have location-specific fiscal information readily available. The Libraries are required to report fiscal activity to the University administration in the budgeting terminology used by the University. Finally, successful management of the materials budget by Acquisitions requires timely information at all fiscal levels.

In addition to Account, Type, Location, and the other fiscal summary reports, FACS also contains foreign currency exchange rates, updated weekly from information published in the *Wall Street Journal*. A simple calculator function in FACS enables any authorized user to determine, for example, the present U.S. equivalent of 35 British pounds or 9,500 Italian lire. During a fiscal transaction, staff can invoke the calculator function by inputting the appropriate ISO country code, and FACS will record the transaction in both the foreign currency and U.S. dollars. Each week the system recalculates encumbrances according the latest exchange rates. It also tracks currency fluctuations by recording previous, highest, and lowest rates in addition to the current rate for each currency.

The currency conversion function is an obvious boon to Acquisitions staff, since it relieves them of time-consuming and error-prone sessions with desk calculators when processing foreign orders and receipts. In addition, the tracking of currency fluctuations enables Libraries management to anticipate the budgetary impact of international currency exchange rates and to provide University administration with more accurate cost projections. The calculator function proved so popular among collection development faculty that public services areas requested access to FACS to help them with ready reference questions about exchange rates. Unfortunately, ready reference access to FACS is presently incompatible with the confidentiality of budget information and with system security, but the request will be re-examined in the future when LCS is able to address FACS upgrades.[9]

A final feature of FACS is called FAIRS, Fund Accounting Information Report System. FACS users authorized for FAIRS can enter a library of pre-programmed management reports, select reports that meet their needs, and run the programs. Output is provided either by printing at the microcomputer work station, by downloading into a spreadsheet file, or by downloading to the Libraries' line printer. In addition, users can program their own reports if their needs are not met by the pre-programmed library of reports.

ONGOING EVALUATIONS

The March 1990 release of FACS was successful: users have not found it necessary to inundate FAIT with questions or complaints, nor have they expressed a preference for the Quattro-generated balance sheets previously provided by Acquisitions. Many campuses took advantage of the opportunity to design complex account structures that accurately reflect collection development priorities.

Even though formal operational evaluation of FACS ceased in the spring of 1990, staff in Acquisitions continue to monitor their own use of the system through transaction logs and periodic reconciliation of account balances. Acquisitions also worked closely with LCS and Library Accounting to guide FACS and its users through the first end-of-year close-out.

FAIT continues to play an important role in system evaluation. FAIRS, the Fund Accounting Information Report System, was held back from the general March 1990 FACS release because it was still under development and had not been fully tested. FAIT advised Acquisitions during FAIRS operational testing and eventual release to all user groups.

FAIT is also guiding Acquisitions through a test of the Categories feature, which was likewise withheld from the general March 1990 release. Since using Categories during fiscal transactions greatly increases the number of keystrokes, Acquisitions must weigh its own needs for operational efficiency against selectors' strongly expressed desire for the enhanced expenditure analysis that Categories provide. FAIT is coordinating a pilot test by selected University Park and branch campus locations to determine the impact of Categories on Acquisitions' operations and their usefulness to subject specialists.

CONCLUSION

The PSUL Acquisitions Department's ability to serve constituent groups has been enhanced by FACS. Designing and implementing FACS involved several types of evaluation: informal appraisal of Acquisitions' services by "client groups," self-assessment by Acquisitions, and formal system evaluation by the Fund Accounting Implementation Team. FACS implementation succeeded because of the service commitment of the Acquisitions Department, the cooperative efforts of representatives from various constituencies, and continual assessment of the system's performance and impact on all users. We anticipate that development of the full LIAS acquisitions system will improve similar cooperative evaluation of Acquisitions' services to the PSUL community.

NOTES

1. Chamberlain, Carol E. "Automating Acquisitions: A Perspective from the Inside," *Library Hi Tech* 3(3):57-68 (issue 11, 1985), p. 58.
2. Cline, Nancy. "LIAS — Library Automation With An Integrated Design," *Library Hi Tech* 1(2):33-48 (Fall 1983).
3. Carson, Sylvia MacKinnon. "LIAS: Online Catalog at Penn State University." *Cataloging & Classification Quarterly* 4(2):1-15 (Winter 1983).
4. Chamberlain, p. 59.
5. Needs have been listed in general terms. The list is not exhaustive; it illustrates the basic kinds of needs which are easily identifiable and tabulated. For the purposes of this table, all faculty with collection development responsibilities, including administrators, library selectors, and head campus librarians were treated as one constituent group called "Collection Development."
6. Campuses were indirectly represented on FAIT by Acquisitions and Accounting, a reasonable mechanism given PSUL's centralized purchasing, and the need for constant, intense consultation throughout the implementation phase. Collection development interests were represented by the faculty on the Implementation Team; all were library selectors.
7. "FACS Reference Manual." Library Computing Services, Pennsylvania State University, March 1990, p. 5.

8. PSUL staff terminals are IBM XT's and PS/s's with resident LIAS connections, a hard drive manager, gateways to Faxon, Telenet, Keydial, and various resident software applications. The general public accesses LIAS via search-only terminals or by dial-up access. Functions such as cataloging, accounting, and electronic mail are available only to authorized Libraries faculty and staff on the IBM's.

9. One of the complications encountered in planning and implementing FACS was the need of LCS to devote considerable time and attention to competing projects, not the least of which was planning for migrating the entire LIAS system from Honeywell to DEC equipment by June 1990.